Kemetic Magic

The Ultimate Guide to Ancient Egyptian Ritual, Kemetic Spirituality, Heka, and the Secrets of the Neteru

© Copyright 2025 - All rights reserved.

The content contained within this book may not be reproduced, duplicated, or transmitted without direct written permission from the author or the publisher.

Under no circumstances will any blame or legal responsibility be held against the publisher or author for any damages, reparation, or monetary loss due to the information contained within this book, either directly or indirectly.

Legal Notice:

This book is copyright-protected. It is only for personal use. You cannot amend, distribute, sell, use, quote, or paraphrase any part of the content within this book without the consent of the author or publisher.

Disclaimer Notice:

Please note the information contained within this document is for educational and entertainment purposes only. All effort has been executed to present accurate, up-to-date, reliable, and complete information. No warranties of any kind are declared or implied. Readers acknowledge that the author is not engaging in the rendering of legal, financial, medical, or professional advice. The content within this book has been derived from various sources. Please consult a licensed professional before attempting any techniques outlined in this book.

By reading this document, the reader agrees that under no circumstances is the author responsible for any losses, direct or indirect, that are incurred as a result of the use of the information contained within this document, including, but not limited to, errors, omissions, or inaccuracies.

Your Free Gift
(only available for a limited time)

Thanks for getting this book! If you want to learn more about various spirituality topics, then join Mari Silva's community and get a free guided meditation MP3 for awakening your third eye. This guided meditation mp3 is designed to open and strengthen ones third eye so you can experience a higher state of consciousness. Simply visit the link below the image to get started.

https://spiritualityspot.com/meditation

Or, Scan the QR code!

Table of Contents

INTRODUCTION 1
CHAPTER 1: THE ORIGINS OF KEMETIC MAGIC 3
CHAPTER 2: SACRED TOOLS OF KEMETIC MAGIC 12
CHAPTER 3: THE NETERU: KEMETIC DEITIES AND THEIR STORIES 36
CHAPTER 4: THE POWER OF HEKA 59
CHAPTER 5: KEY KEMETIC RITUALS 74
CHAPTER 6: MYSTERIES OF LIFE, DEATH, AND REBIRTH 88
CHAPTER 7: ADVANCED KEMETIC MAGIC PRACTICES 102
CHAPTER 8: LIVING IN ALIGNMENT WITH MA'AT 119
CHAPTER 9: PRESERVING KEMETIC WISDOM FOR THE FUTURE 130
APPENDIX: KEMETIC MAGIC GLOSSARY 137
HERE'S ANOTHER BOOK BY MARI SILVA THAT YOU MIGHT LIKE...... 144
YOUR FREE GIFT (ONLY AVAILABLE FOR A LIMITED TIME) 145
REFERENCES 146
IMAGE SOURCES 152

Introduction

The world is a harsh place. Life gets very confusing. Relationships are complex, and no relationship is as complex as the one we have with ourselves. Everyone has experienced self-doubt, hopelessness, and despair. When a storm rolls through the harbor, any boats that are unanchored or unmoored get swept out to sea. You need something to keep you tethered and offer you a lifeline to survive in this world. Many people turn to religion when they feel lost. There's no better religion to give you that stability than Kemetism.

The Ancient Egyptians ruled the lands along the Nile River for over 3,000 years. They gave us foundational knowledge like timekeeping and calendars. They gave us writing, mathematics, architecture, and engineering. We use their agricultural techniques and irrigation systems. We wouldn't have makeup or cosmetics without them. Their skills in weaving, crafting, and textile production were second to none. Even modern science owes much to the lessons first learned by their healers and priests. Ancient Egypt still has a lot to offer us despite their civilization dying out long ago.

Kemetism honors everything the Ancient Egyptians have given us, and it applies those things to all facets of its religion. The core doctrine of Kemetism preaches many of the same principles and values as the Ancient Egyptian religion. It can make spirituality relevant in an age where technology is worshipped like a god. The key factor in the success of Kemetic beliefs is that there's something for everyone. The Ancient Egyptian pantheon has a massive number of deities that embody an extensive amount of traits, concepts, and powers.

A significant part of Kemetism is its relationship with magic. This doesn't mean you'll be dressing in robes and waving around a wand like a cut-rate Merlin. Kemetic magic is practical. It reinforces the connection between nature and spirituality. You might not learn how to shoot fireballs out of your fingertips, but you *will* learn how the power of fire can be harnessed to manifest beneficial outcomes. It takes time and dedication to reach the point where you can consider yourself a master at Kemetic magic, but it's well worth it in the end.

There is much you can gain from embracing Kemetism. It will enrich your mind and give you a solid foundation to explore your spirituality. You can apply what you learn from Kemetism to every aspect of your life. Your family, friends, hobbies, and career can benefit from the wisdom and insight granted by the divine teachings of the gods. The mysteries of Kemetic magic are yours to discover. Do you want to know how? All you have to do is read on.

Chapter 1: The Origins of Kemetic Magic

Kemetism (also known as Kemeticism) is a neopagan religion that draws heavily upon the religion of Ancient Egypt. It's considered a revival or reconstruction of the original belief system, but with bits and pieces taken from other pagan religions. Most practitioners follow three main branches: Kemetic Orthodoxy, Reconstructed Kemetism, and Syncretic Kemetism. They all share a foundation based on Ancient Egyptian society and a veneration of their numerous deities.

Kemetism draws heavily on Ancient Egyptian society.[1]

Modern Kemetism was first established in the 1970s and 1980s, continuing to gain traction as more people sought alternatives to the traditional Abrahamic and Eastern religions. While most Kemetic practitioners view their religion as a revival or reconstruction of the Ancient Egyptian belief system, some claim direct continuity between their version of Kemetism and the original religion. According to their traditions, secret societies continued to practice their religion, even after paganism was banned in 392 CE by Theodosius I, the emperor of Rome.

Determining the exact number of Kemetists in the world right now is difficult, but it's estimated that there are tens of thousands of practitioners. When the first revivals began popping up in the late-1970s, there were only a few thousand worldwide. Kemetism really started to take hold after Kemetic Orthodoxy (led by the organization known as the House of Netjer) was officially recognized as a religion by the United States in 1994. Interest in Ancient Egypt grew in the late 1990s and early 2000s, thanks to popular depictions in the media, such as the 1999 action film *The Mummy*, the 1998 animated film *The Prince of Egypt*, the 2017 video game *Assassin's Creed Origins*, and the 1995 television miniseries *Moses*.

Many Kemetists are drawn to the religion because of its mystical potential and adherence to balance. They can feel the disharmony in modern civilization, where throngs of people are forced into narrow categories, made dependent on technology, and just fighting to survive. Having a religion that promotes unity and order is attractive to those stuck as cogs in the system. There is chaos all around us, but Kemetism strives to wrangle the turmoil and allow its followers a chance to find peace and happiness in harmony with the powers of the universe.

Kemetism and Ancient Egypt

The name "Kemetism" stems from a set of hieroglyphs found on the western Luxor Obelisk, which is one of a pair of towering monuments erected initially by Ramesses II outside the Luxor Temple in Egypt. The western obelisk was gifted to the French in 1830 and moved to the Place de la Concorde in Paris. It contained the hieroglyphs for the word "Kemet," which was the name used by Ancient Egyptians for their kingdom. They are notated as *"km.t"* in the conventional vocalization and appear on the obelisk as:

The name "Kemet" translates to "black soil," which references the dark, fertile mud left behind when the Nile River flooded the region. Due to the fertile soil, Ancient Egyptians relied heavily on agriculture, farming the lands to cultivate wheat, papyrus, flax, and other crops for trade. This trade, especially wheat, allowed Ancient Egyptians to survive in the famine-prone Middle East, and it was used to develop diplomatic and economic relationships with foreign countries.

Influence of Ancient Egyptian Culture

Ancient Egyptians carried their traditions and beliefs well beyond the confines of their borders. It spread far and wide, leaving an indelible mark on the region. The various iterations of the realm lasted from around 3150 BCE to 30 CE when the Roman Empire annexed Egypt following the deaths of Cleopatra and Mark Antony. Many of the structures built by Ancient Egyptians stand to this day, including their pyramids, temples, and monuments. Their culture has similarly withstood the test of time, and the rise of Kemetism is a testament to that longevity.

Ancient Egyptian Religion

Ancient Egyptians followed a polytheistic religion with more than 1,500 gods, including ones adopted from other cultures and humans raised to divine status. The core of their belief system was based on the connection between their deities and their daily life. Each deity represented aspects of the natural world, universe, elements, abstract forces, and values held by their people. Their deities could manifest in many forms, giving them complex characteristics and various roles in Ancient Egyptian culture.

Part of the Ancient Egyptian religion involved the complicated relationships between the gods. They were often grouped into "families," usually consisting of a mother, father, and child. Multiple gods could be combined into a composite deity through the process of syncretism. The most well-known of these composite deities is Amun-Ra, who was created by combining Amun, the god of air and primeval creation, and Ra, the god of the sun. Syncretic gods were given special status by Ancient Egyptians, and Amun-Ra was made the chief deity during the New Kingdom.

The Neteru

Kemetism uses the term "Neteru" to refer to the pantheon of gods and goddesses from the Ancient Egyptian religion. However, the Neteru are more than just deities - they are divine archetypes and abstract forces that govern the natural world and Ancient Egyptian cosmology. They're inextricably linked to the mechanisms of the universe, infused into every moment of mortal existence. The Neteru are collectively the engine that drives all life forward. Without their power and guidance, mortals would be lost, unable to form relationships or create societies. Each of the Neteru embodies certain principles or abstract forces that they control.

Some branches of Kemetism prefer to use the original Ancient Egyptian names for the gods, such as "Anpu" for *Anubis*, or "*Heru*" for Horus. This is in line with the practices of Kemetic Orthodoxy, which urges followers to avoid using any of the Romanized spellings of names and words associated with the religion. Even the name "Neteru" is written as "Netjeru." In Kemetic Orthodoxy, there is a single divine cosmological force known as Netjer, which is the syncretic collective of interlinked gods and goddesses, as well as their combined associated concepts.

Heka and Magic

Heka is both a god and a concept in the Ancient Egyptian belief system. As a god, he represents magic and medicine. Heka can also be used to describe the practice of magical rituals. During the Old Kingdom, Heka was the supernatural energy possessed by the gods. The pharaoh, who was said to become a god upon their ascension to the throne, was expected to "cannibalize" other gods in order to gain their magical power. Eventually, Heka developed into a deity who was worshipped by the cults established in his name. During the Ptolemaic Dynasty, Heka was given the responsibility of proclaiming a new pharaoh as the son of Isis, elevating them to divine status.

Many ancient medical texts written by priests and healers invoke the power of Heka as a means to cure diseases and other ailments. Ancient Egyptians believed that diseases had supernatural origins and, therefore, could be thwarted by magic. They practiced rituals using spell recitations and amulets to call on the power of Heka. These rituals were believed to bring protection and healing to the mind, body, and spirit. There were also rituals meant to help guide the souls of the dead to their proper afterlife. The magical energy was seen as something inherent to the universe, being woven into the very fabric of existence.

Heka was usually depicted wearing an ornate hemhem crown - a ceremonial headgear made of a triple atef, two urei, two horns of a ram, and six solar disks - and a sidelock that indicated he was a legitimate heir of Osiris. He would be carrying an ankh, also known as the "key of life," which symbolized life-giving substances like water and air. It could also be used to bring souls into the afterlife. Along with the ankh would be a crook and flail, the emblem of a pharaoh's authority. The crook represented kingship, while the flail embodied the land's fertility and the harvest's bounty.

The Egyptian god Heka.²

Ma'at and Ancient Egyptian Cosmology

Ma'at (or "maat"), like Heka, was both a deity and a concept. She is the goddess of truth, justice, law, morality, harmony, and order. It was said that she brought order to the chaos upon the moment of creation.

Ma'at is responsible for regulating the seasons, stars, and actions of mortals. She was usually depicted with an ostrich feather strapped to her head. The feather would be weighed against the souls of the departed. Her judgment on the balance between the feather and soul decided whether they would move on to paradise in the Kingdom of Osiris or be devoured by Ammit and forever destroyed.

The concept of maat was the principles of truth, honor, and justice. The people of Ancient Egypt were expected to live their daily lives by embodying these principles, especially when interacting with their family, community, environment, country, and deities. As Egyptian law was

The Egyptian goddess Ma'at.⁹

established as an institution, the pharaoh and arbiter of justice was known as the "Lord of Maat." As long as the pharaoh lived by these tenets, the kingdom would prosper. If they failed to live up to those expectations, they would be possessed by Isfet, the embodiment of chaos, injustice, violence, and lies.

When Ancient Egyptians performed any rites or rituals, they needed to align with maat. Every part of the ceremony had to remain balanced. If the rituals disrupted the balance of the world, they were deemed evil and an invitation for ill-intentioned spirits. Those who intentionally performed unbalanced rituals were shunned from society and seen as marked for doom. Following the principles of maat in a ritual was the only way to achieve positive results.

Ancient Egyptian Creation Myths

According to the Pyramid Texts, decorations on the walls of tombs, and various other ancient writings, there are multiple versions of the Ancient Egyptian creation myth. The oldest of these myths credited the god Ra with the creation of the world. His emergence from chaos gave rise to Shu, who represented air, and his counterpart Tefnut, who represented moisture. Their union resulted in Geb, the god of the earth, and Nut, the goddess of the sky. Geb and Nut then begat Osiris, Set, Isis, and Nephthys.

Later additions to the myths involved a dramatic confrontation between Horus and Set. In the tale, Set murders Osiris and attempts to claim the kingship of the world, as well as Isis, the consort of Osiris. Horus, the son of Osiris and Isis, challenges Set, ultimately prevailing and taking his rightful place on the throne. These myths helped to give the people of Ancient Egypt ideals to emulate and were a powerful link between the kingship of the gods and the mortal pharaohs.

There are four different versions of the creation myth that originated from four of Ancient Egypt's major cities: Heliopolis, Hermopolis, Memphis, and Thebes.

All of them share certain elements, such as the belief that the world emerged from Nu, the lifeless waters of chaos. A pyramid-like mound called the "benben" rose from the waters, and the sun first appeared from that mound. Various iterations of the story equate the sun with the gods Ra or Khepri, a lotus flower, and different animals, such as a falcon, heron, scarab beetle, or a human child.

1. Heliopolis Creation Myth

The Heliopolis creation myth was centered around the god Atum, who was claimed to have existed within the waters of Nu as an inert being. Atum appeared from the benben and spawned Shu and Tefnut by way of a sneeze. The other major gods were created by Shu and Tefnut's coupling, bringing the total to nine deities. They were collectively known as the Ennead, with Atum positioned as their chief.

2. Hermopolis Creation Myth

In the Hermopolis creation myth, the stories were primarily set in the time before the creation of the world. Eight deities represented the primordial waters, and together, they were called the Ogdoad. They included Nu and his female counterpart, Naunet, who embodied the lifeless water itself; Hauhet and her male counterpart, Huh, who personified the infinite reach of the water; Kek and Kauket, who symbolized the darkness held within the water; and Amun and Amaunet, who were the manifestation of the hidden and unknowable nature of the water.

The Ogdoad was divided into an equal number of male and female deities. They were depicted as aquatic animals that dwelled within the waters, with the females shown as snakes and the males as frogs. When these two sides came together, it resulted in a cataclysmic event, causing the benben to rise from the water. From the benben came the sun, and when it ascended into the sky, it bathed the world in light. The Ogdoad were then responsible for bringing life to the world, eventually creating humanity.

3. Memphis Creation Myth

The Memphis creation myth used the motif of craftsmanship to explain the origins of the world. They held that a supreme being thought and spoke the god Ptah into existence. Ptah was the patron god of artisans, and he possessed the ability to spark an idea, envision the final product, and use his skills to shape raw materials, turning the concept into reality. Ptah forged the other gods and the rest of the world by cultivating an idea in his heart and speaking the names of those things out loud. The Memphis myth was able to coexist with the Heliopolis myth, as they believed it was Ptah who gave form to Atum and the Ennead.

4. Thebes Creation Myth

The god Amun was at the core of the Thebes creation myth. He was still a member of the Ogdoad, but also held the position as their chief deity. It was said that Amun was responsible for the creation of everything, being the hidden force that brought the world, the gods, the elements, and nature into existence. Amun was an amalgamation of all other creation stories, serving as their personification and transcending by being "beyond the sky and deeper than the underworld." He called both the Ogdoad and the Ennead into being by breaking the stillness of the primordial waters and allowing them to take shape. As Thebes evolved into the kingdom's religious capital, Amun overtook the other gods to become the pantheon's supreme deity.

The Duat and the Afterlife

The *Duat* is the name for the underworld in Ancient Egyptian mythology. Newly departed souls would awaken there, and they would face a number of challenges on their way to a paradise realm where they could rest peacefully for all eternity. Failure to overcome those challenges would result in the complete annihilation of the soul, removing it from existence. Along their journey across the Duat, the souls had to traverse through multiple gates before reaching the Hall of Truth, where the "Weighing of the Heart" ritual was performed.

Those whose souls were deemed to be in balance were permitted to pass into A'aru or the Field of Reeds. A'aru was a paradise realm where the souls were reunited with their loved ones who were also worthy of reward, and together, they could live happily for all eternity without pain, fear, or sorrow. The Field of Reeds was part of the Kingdom of Osiris, and he held dominion over both death and rebirth. The souls that weren't worthy of A'aru were cast into the fiery pits of Ammit, who tormented the souls before devouring them.

Ancient Egyptian Magical Practices

In Ancient Egypt, magical practices weren't the exclusive domain of pharaohs and priests. Everyday citizens were just as capable of performing magical rituals for a variety of reasons. Merchants, artisans, and farmers would use amulets, charms, and basic rituals to protect their families, ensure healthy crops, and bring them good fortune. They could also use heka to help with illnesses and injuries, invoking the magic alongside practical medicines and treatments. Women would wear fertility amulets and perform rituals to aid with having children.

Magic was viewed as something that was as much a part of the world as the wind, rivers, or fire. It was a part of the people's daily lives. Ancient Egyptian priests were the conduits through which ordinary citizens could commune with the gods. The priests were responsible for maintaining the temples dedicated to their deities. When citizens required direct communication with the gods, they could go to the temples and get the assistance of the priests. The priests would also perform rituals for the good of the kingdom, utilizing magic for widespread results.

Chapter 2: Sacred Tools of Kemetic Magic

Those who practice Kemetic magic must have a collection of sacred tools to assist in their rituals and spellcasting. The tools are used as a conduit to send and receive the divine energy of the gods and the elements. Every practitioner of Kemetism should build their own collection of sacred tools that have special significance to them. These tools are not something you can simply go out and buy; you have to look for tools you feel a connection with. The tools meant for you will seek you out and speak to you on a metaphysical level. You will know them when you see them and feel the synchronicity of the vibrations between you and the right tools.

Sacred Tools of Ancient Egypt

Ancient Egyptians used sacred tools for their rituals, just like modern-day followers of Kemetism. Each of their tools had both a practical function and a special symbolic meaning. The people of Ancient Egypt held their tools in reverence, keeping the sacred objects in a place of honor in their homes. They would choose which tools to use based on the specific ritual being performed. The chosen sacred tool needed to be representative of the ritual's intention, as well as the type of magic being used. They were often one of the following items:

Crook and Flail

The crook and flail were frequently depicted in the hands of various gods, especially Osiris. The crook was shaped like a shepherd's staff and represented the authority of the pharaoh and kingship over the lands. The flail was an agricultural tool whose purpose was to separate grains from their husks. It represented the fertility of the earth and the people of Ancient Egypt. Together, the crook and flail were a badge of high station, and they were a symbol of the balance between leaders and their flocks.

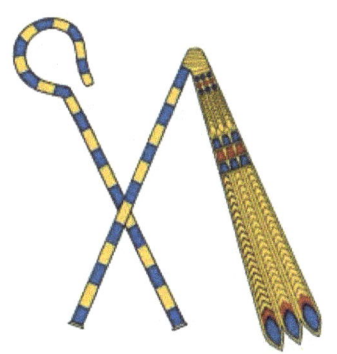

Crook and flail.[4]

Amulet

Amulets were frequently worn by Ancient Egyptians, and they could also be used as a sacred tool in magical rituals. It was believed they could bring good luck. They were made to look like the gods, sacred animals, or other significant symbols. Wearing an amulet was meant to confer power and protection to the wearer. Different types of amulet shapes were connected to different magical effects, such as healing, strength, longevity, or fertility.

Heart Scarab of Hatnefer.[5]

Scarab

The scarab was a symbol connected to the sun god Ra. Sacred tools could either be objects created in the shape of a scarab or the empty shells of real scarab beetles. Scarabs represented change and metamorphosis, just like how the living beetles laid eggs that transformed into adults. The sun also changed by moving across the sky and disappearing beneath the horizon. The wings of the scarab looked like a dazzling sunset when reflected in the light. This added to their mystique and gave them an otherworldly quality.

The Scarab.[6]

Fetish

Imiut fetishes were used by Ancient Egyptians as sacred tools in their funerary rituals. They were made by securing an animal skin to a long pole that was set in a bowl or vase as a base. The fetishes were usually connected to Anubis or Osiris, and their presence in rituals was meant to help guide the souls of the dead into the next world. Most fetishes used the skin from a bull or large feline, transferring the power of the animal to the magic of the ritual. After the completion of the ritual, the fetishes were either placed alongside the mummified body or removed to a shrine and put in a place of honor.

Imiut Fetish.[7]

Sistrum

The sistrum was a percussion instrument used by Ancient Egyptians to create a rhythmic clanking or jangling sound. It was often used in rituals and ceremonies dedicated to the goddesses Hathor or Bat. Sistrums were an instrument exclusive to women, typically musical priestesses who used them for religious practices. However, on special occasions, the pharaoh would play the sistrum, especially when making an offering to Hathor. They were an essential sacred tool for healing rituals, and their rhythmic sounds were believed to help the people connect to their deities.

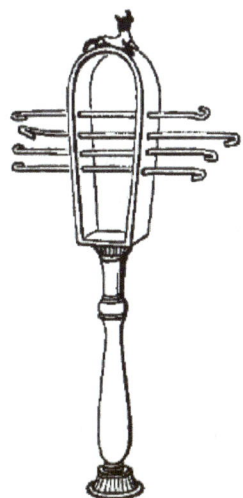

Ancient Egyptian Sistrum.[9]

The Lamp

Earthenware lamp.[9]

A lamp could be used as a sacred tool in rituals, as the light was believed to ward off evil spirits. Lamps would be lit and placed around the space where the ritual was taking place. Once the lamps were lit, the person performing the ritual would have to recite a prayer to the gods, asking for their protection. The power of the gods would flow through the flame of the lamp, spreading its warmth and light, keeping any ill-intentioned beings from interrupting the ritual and throwing it off-balance.

Lotus Flower

The lotus flower was a symbol of creation, reincarnation, and the sun. This was due to the fact that lotus petals often close at night and open during the day, connecting them with the movement of the sun and the idea of rebirth. The lotus was also known as "sensen" and was a regular component of the Ancient Egyptian people's daily rituals. It also represented Osiris sitting on his throne, which had mystical connotations based on its connection to the goddess Nephthys, who represented mysticism and repose.

Nemes

A nemes was a headdress consisting of several headcloths adorned with stripes, flaps, and sometimes an icon representing a deity. It was a sacred tool of Ancient Egyptian pharaohs, and was a common piece of iconography in depictions of the gods. The nemes were used in religious rituals to call upon the power and strength of the ancient kings. It can famously be seen on the statue of the Great Sphinx of Giza.

Ancient Egyptian Nemes.[10]

Gold, Silver, and Gemstones

Ancient Egyptians believed that the skin of their gods was made of gold and that the gods' bones were made of silver. Using gold or silver items as sacred tools during rituals would have helped them connect physically to their deities. Gemstones like lapis lazuli, rubies, and diamonds were also considered to be part of the gods' physical forms, and their dazzling beauty would catch the attention of the forces being invoked by the rituals.

Knots and Numbers

Knots represented a convergence of multiple natural or elemental forces. The reef knot was depicted in Ancient Egyptian hieroglyphs, and knots were a common decorative element, often appearing on necklaces, brooches, and amulets. During a ritual, a knot or depiction of a knot was meant to encourage the cooperation of different magical forces in leading to the desired outcome. Numbers were also used to invoke mystical power, with the numeral "7" (depicted by Ancient Egyptians as four lines above three lines) being particularly noted for its connection to effectiveness and totality.

Feather of Ma'at

The Feather of Ma'at was a representation of the ostrich feather worn by the goddess Ma'at, which was used during the Weighing of the Heart ceremony. When Ancient Egyptians used the feather as a sacred tool in rituals, it was meant to embody truth, justice, and balance. Although any type of feather could stand in as a facsimile of Ma'at's feather, it was believed that using an actual ostrich feather had a better chance of making the ritual succeed to its intended degree.

Eye of Horus

The Eye of Horus, also known as the "left *wedjat* eye" (as opposed to the Eye of Ra, or right wedjat eye), was a symbol that conveyed powers of protection, healing, and royal authority. In the myth concerning the power struggle between Horus and Set, Horus had his eye(s) torn out by his rival. The eye was eventually healed and returned to Horus, who gave it to

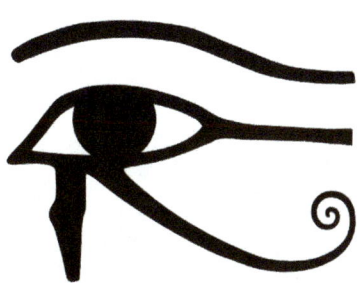

Eye of Horus.[11]

his dead father, Osiris, which helped sustain him in the afterlife. The Eye of Horus was often used as a sacred tool during funerary rites. When it was paired with the Eye of Ra, the latter represented the sun, while the former represented the moon.

The Girdle of Isis.[12]

Girdle of Isis

The Girdle of Isis, also called the "tyet," was an Ancient Egyptian symbol using looped knots to represent the goddess Isis. The loops somewhat resemble cloth bandages, tying into the healing power of Isis. She was the wife of Osiris and mother of Horus and had control over certain aspects of the natural world. It was also believed that she possessed more magical power than any other deity. Sacred tools using the Girdle of Isis were typically in the form of amulets carved from a red stone or gem.

Ushabti

Ushabti of Ramesses IV.[18]

A *ushabti* was a burial figurine used by Ancient Egyptians as a sacred tool in funerary rituals. They believed that the figures depicted by the ushabtis would act as servants to the dead in the afterlife. Many ushabtis were shown bearing a basket on their backs and a hoe on their shoulder, indicating that they were ready and willing to do any manual labor required of them. They often had hieroglyphs inscribed along their legs that expressed how eager they were to work.

Uraeus

The Uraeus was a stylized Egyptian cobra depicted in an upright position. It was a popular symbol of royalty, sovereignty, and divine authority. Many pharaohs and deities were shown wearing the Uraeus as part of their headdress. The name "Uraeus" translates to "rearing cobra," and it gave the appearance of a venomous snake ready to strike. Sacred tools in the form of the Uraeus included statuettes, figurines, and amulets. They were used in rituals that beseeched the gods, kings, and pharaohs for help.

The Uraeus (Rearing Egyptian Cobra).[14]

Letters to the Dead

A common ritual practice in Ancient Egypt included writing letters to the deceased. It was believed that these letters could reach the dead friends and family in the afterlife. The dead would then decide whether or not to grant the requests for aid or advice contained in the letters. The letters to the dead needed to be burned during the ritual in order for them to reach their intended recipients in the afterlife. Reading letters written by others was also considered bad form and could result in a curse upon the reader.

Letter Written in Hieratic Script on Papyrus.[15]

Kemetic Symbols of Power

There are three major Kemetic symbols of power: the ankh, the was-scepter, and the djed pillar. As representations of overarching concepts, they provide those who use these symbols with an inherent set of traits derived from Ancient Egyptian religious beliefs. The iconography of the ankh, was-scepter, and djed pillar can further be seen as a systematic confirmation of the powers derived from the forces and deities associated with each symbol. They could be used for a variety of purposes, including magical rituals, religious ceremonies, hieroglyphic inscriptions, clothing ornamentation, decorations, and artwork.

Ankh

The ankh was a common symbol of power used in Ancient Egyptian rituals and decorations. It represents life and rebirth, which were both very important to the people of Ancient Egypt. The ankh's shape is reminiscent of a human body. Its horizontal bar looks like outstretched arms, and the vertical bar mimics a person standing straight. The loop at the top is similar to a human head. The ankh symbolizes the energy of the physical body. It's also believed that the bottom "T" section represents masculine energy, while the loop represents feminine energy. The pair coming together and connecting is meant to show how males and females can unite as a single being.

Ankh.[16]

Was-Scepter

The was-scepter is a symbol of power and domination in Kemetism. It was originally used to capture poisonous snakes in Ancient Egypt, but it was eventually reserved as an implement by the gods. The was-scepter has a straight staff with a curved head that is often carved in the form of an animal head. One of the most popular choices of the animal head is the "sha," or Set animal, which is the jackal-like creature depicted as the head of the god Set. Both Set and Anubis are typically shown wielding the was-scepter as an expression of their authority over the mortal world.

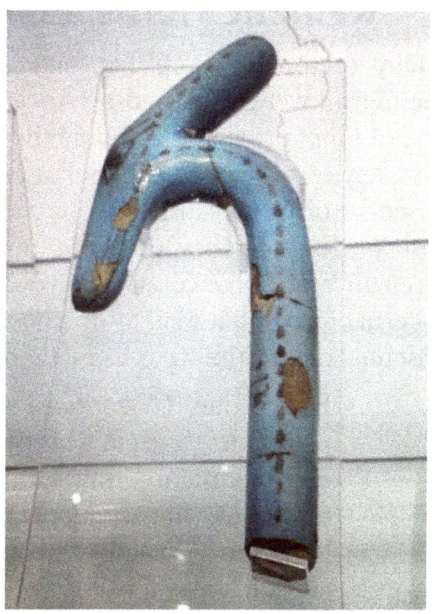

Was-Scepter.[17]

Djed Pillar.[18]

Djed Pillar

The Djed Pillar is a symbol of power that represents strength and stability. Ancient Egyptians used the djed pillar as a symbolic depiction of the backbone of Osiris, and it could also be associated with the creator god Ptah. It was used in a ceremony called "raising the djed," which was part of the Ancient Egyptian jubilee celebration known as the Sed festival. The ceremony was meant to ask for the gods' blessing at the start of the agricultural season, providing that year's crops with protection and healthy growth.

Kemetic Herbs, Plants, and Essential Oils

Many of the herbs, plants, and essential oils used by practitioners of Kemetism were also used by Ancient Egyptians. They have withstood the test of time, proving that the medicinal qualities they possess are useful for a variety of maladies. The toolkit of Kemetism includes herbs, plants, and essential oils that can heal your mental, emotional, and spiritual ailments just as much as they can your physical injuries. They can also provide strength and enhancement to your natural abilities or protect you from external forces that wish to do you harm. Here's a list of herbs, plants, and essential oils common in Kemetic ritual toolkits:

- **Blue Lotus (*Nymphaea nouchali* var. *caerulea*):** An important plant in Ancient Egyptian culture that symbolizes purity, enlightenment, transformation, and divine beauty. It also represents transcendence and a spiritual awakening. The blue lotus can be used to treat anxiety and serve as a sleep aid. The alkaloid known as *aporphine* can be found in blue lotus flowers, which is a natural remedy for erectile dysfunction and was used by Ancient Egyptians as an aphrodisiac.

Blue Lotus Flower in a Pond.[19]

- **Frankincense (*Olibanum*):** An aromatic resin frequently used in incense, perfumes, lotions, and soaps that comes from *Boswellia* trees. In Ancient Egypt, it symbolized divinity, purification, and the afterlife. It was used by Ancient Egyptians in the mummification process to clean out various cavities of the body. Frankincense essential oils can help to reduce pain and inflammation, kill germs and bacteria, aid with deep breathing, and have even been shown to fight cancerous cells.

Frankincense.[20]

- **Garlic (*Allium sativum*):** A bulbous flowering vegetable plant used as a cooking ingredient and aromatic. Ancient Egyptians believed it boosted a person's energy and endurance, which made it popular among laborers, such as those who helped to construct the pyramids. It symbolizes strength, vitality, and protection. The scent of garlic is said to ward off evil spirits and prevent illnesses.

Raw Garlic Bulbs and Cloves.[21]

- **Aloe** (*Aloe vera*): A flowering succulent plant whose leaves contain a gel that can be used for medicinal purposes. Aloe vera has been used by many different cultures since ancient times to treat wounds and can serve as an ingredient in cosmetics. Ancient Egyptians called it the "plant of immortality," as it was believed to have youth-restorative properties. It was a well-known part of the beauty regimens of Ancient Egyptian queens Cleopatra and Nefertiti.

Aloe Vera Houseplant.[22]

- **Thyme** (*Thymus*): A culinary herb that can also be used for medicinal and ornamental purposes. Ancient Egyptians used thyme as part of the embalming process, and they burned it as an offering to the gods. It symbolizes courage, good fortune, and purification. Thyme has anti-inflammatory and antibacterial properties and has been used to treat yeast infections, fungal skin diseases, and high blood pressure.

Bundle of Thyme.[23]

- **Myrrh**: An aromatic resin extracted from a handful of thorny trees in the *Commiphora* genus, such as the African myrrh (*Commiphora myrrha*) tree. It has been used to make medicine, incense, and perfumes throughout history. Several ancient cultures mixed it with wine as an analgesic to induce a state of euphoria. Ancient Egyptians considered it a bridge between the mortal world and the afterlife. It was a major ingredient in the embalming process, as it helped to prevent decay in mummified bodies.

Myrrh Resin.[34]

- **Fennel (*Foeniculum vulgare*)**: A flowering plant and perennial herb that is a popular culinary ingredient and medicinal aid. Fennel symbolizes protection, longevity, and strength. In Ancient Egypt, fennel seeds were chewed after meals to aid with digestion, and juice from certain varieties was used as a natural contraceptive. It has also been used to treat snake bites, eye ailments, and respiratory issues.

Fennel Plants with Flowering Heads.[25]

- **Licorice (*Glycyrrhiza glabra*):** A flowering legume plant that can be used for culinary flavoring, medicinal ingredients, or as a dietary supplement. It symbolizes health, rebirth, and the afterlife. Large amounts of licorice were found in the tomb of the pharaoh Tutankhamun (King Tut) when it was rediscovered in 1922. Ancient Egyptians brewed licorice root in teas, and eating the plant provided them with relief from digestive, eye, and skin conditions.

Dried Licorice Roots.[26]

- **Roman Chamomile (*Chamaemelum nobile*):** A low perennial plant native to Northwest Africa and Western Europe that is one of two species typically known as chamomile, the other being *Matricaria chamomilla* or German chamomile. It symbolizes rebirth, regeneration, patience, and the divine. Ancient Egyptians connected chamomile to the sun god Ra, and they burned dried leaves from the plant as an offering to their gods and ancestors. Chamomile oil was used to anoint the bodies of the dead during burial rituals, protecting the departed souls and helping their rebirth in the afterlife.

Roman Chamomile Plants.[27]

Sacred Colors of Kemetism

The sacred colors of Kemetism are the same as the color palette used by Ancient Egyptians: red, yellow, blue, green, black, and white. The limitation in available dyes resulted in the distinctive primary color scheme seen in lots of Ancient Egyptian clothing, jewelry, and decor. Each color is associated with a major deity, elemental force, and precious gem or metal, and they carry symbolic connotations that connect to the forces they represent. Here's a table with the sacred colors and what they mean:

Color	**Red**	**Yellow**	**Blue**	**Green**	**Black**	White
Symbolism	Passion, vitality, chaos	Sun, divinity, eternity	Heavens, creation, divine	Life, growth, renewal	Death, fertility, resurrection	Purity, sanctity, clarity
Elemental Force	Blood	Fire	Air	Nature	Earth	Water
Precious Gem/Metal	Carnelian	Gold	Lapis Lazuli	Malachite	Onyx	Silver
Associated God	Set	Ra	Horus	Osiris	Anubis	Isis

Magical Hieroglyphic Symbols

Ancient Egyptian hieroglyphs were stylized pictures used to express words, sounds, thoughts, ideas, abstract concepts, and beliefs. They could also be used to record events, stories, and historical accounts in written form, preserved for the ages on the walls of temples and tombs. The exact form Egyptian hieroglyphs take can vary from one historical period to another, but the core meanings usually remain the same. Kemetism employs hieroglyphs to aid in magical rituals, utilizing their intrinsic power and symbolism to guide the ceremony in the right direction. Here's a brief list of some more popular hieroglyphs and what they represent:

- **Scarab:** Represents creation, resurrection, and the cycle of life.

- **Lotus:** Represents purity, renewal, and the day/night cycle.

- **Crook:** Represents kingship, protection, and leadership.

- **Flail:** Represents fertility, prosperity, and control over nature.

- **Ankh:** Represents life, the afterlife, and divine power.

- **Duat:** Represents the underworld, afterlife, and death.

- **Seba:** Represents stars, constellations, and the underworld.

- **Eye of Horus:** Represents health, protection, and restoration.

- **Eye of Ra:** Represents vigilance, balance, and divine protection.

- **Djet Pillar:** Represents stability, strength, and endurance.

- **Was Scepter:** Represents order, control, and dominion.

- **Cartouche:** Represents good luck, royalty, and protection from evil.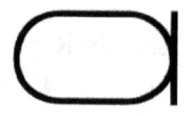

- **Scale:** Represents justice, balance, and the Weighing of the Heart ritual.

- **Owl:** Represents wisdom, intuition, and awareness.

- **Goat:** Represents dignity, status, and fertility.

- **Sistrum:** Represents joy, love, and music.

- **Khopesh:** Represents might, conquest, and military prowess.

Ritual Outfits and Adornments

Kemetism takes after its Ancient Egyptian predecessor by having relatively simple ceremonial regalia for practitioners to don when performing a ritual. Most practitioners wear a white linen or cotton robe to signify their purity of spirit and intentions. Don't use any wool or leather, as they're considered taboo. Basic ornamentation can indicate rank or ceremonial role. Clean, white clothing can also be worn, as long as it's something simple, like a tunic or dress.

In addition to robes and clothing, many Kemetism practitioners will wear sacred adornments, like headdresses, amulets, necklaces, pendants, earrings, bracelets, rings, and other jewelry. These are meant to confer magical protections to the wearer and allow them to establish a connection to the gods, the elements, and the natural world. Each piece should hold special significance to the wearer rather than just for the sake of spectacle. The designs of sacred adornments help to express their meaning through the use of shapes, colors, materials, and hieroglyphs.

Ancient Egyptian Jewelry.[28]

Finger Ring with Ptah Hieroglyph.[29]

Ancient Egyptian Necklace.[30]

Ancient Egyptian Diadem.[31]

Practical Exercises

Try out these Kemetic exercises to show off what you've learned and help reinforce the practices of the religion:

Kemetic Cleansing Ritual

This ritual will help you cleanse and purify your sacred space. Here's what you'll need:

- 1 Candle
- 1 Item of offering (a piece of fresh fruit or slice of whole grain bread)
- 1 Offering vessel (bowl or basin)
- Sea Salt
- Incense (frankincense or myrrh)
- Matches or a lighter
- A clean space

To perform this cleansing ritual, follow these steps:
1. Start off by setting your boundary. You can do this by spreading the sea salt in a circle around your intended sacred space.
2. Place the candle on your altar or in the middle of your salt circle. Use a match or your lighter to light the candle.
3. Set your bowl or basin in front of the lit candle. Make sure it's clean and dry.
4. Light your incense, let it burn for a few seconds, and then blow it out.
5. Holding the incense in your hand, move it across your sacred space. Start at the north position, then move it to the south, then east, and finally, west. When you're finished, put the incense down.
6. Close your eyes and visualize your sacred space as being clean and pure.
7. Make known your intention by reciting it out loud. Say, "I intend to cleanse this sacred space and purify it for future rituals."
8. Put your offering item into the offering vessel.
9. Say, "I call on Kebechet, daughter of Anubis and goddess of purification. Grant me the power to cleanse this space and make it sacred."
10. Prostrate yourself before the candle and offering vessel, stretching your arms out over your head. Lift your head and arms to the sky, and then bring them back down.
11. Repeat this action seven times.
12. When you are done, say, "Kebechet, I close this cleansing ritual. Thank you for your power and grace."
13. Blow out your candle.

That's the end of the cleansing ritual. You now have purified your sacred space, and it can be used to perform other Kemetic rituals in the future.

Building Your Kemetic Altar

Having an altar for your Kemetic rituals is a huge boon. It cuts down on prep time and gives you a permanent sacred space. While some altars can become quite ornate, you can build a basic one to start. As you become more immersed in Kemetism, you can expand your altar and add special flourishes to really personalize it.

This is what you'll need to build your first Kemetic altar:

- Image of chosen god or goddess
- Candle
- Offering vessel
- Incense/essential oils diffuser
- Linen cloth
- Platform

Just follow these steps to build the altar:

1. The first thing you need to do is set up your platform. This is the base of your altar. It can be something like a table, desk, shelf, or even just a box. Place it somewhere that you can easily access but won't get in the way of your normal activities.
2. Drape the cloth over your platform. You can choose a cloth of any color, but it helps to use a color connected to your god or goddess.
3. Set the candle in the middle of the altar.
4. Place the image of your god or goddess behind the candle. The image can be a figurine, woodcarving, statuette, or a drawn, painted, or printed-out picture of your chosen deity.
5. Put the offering vessel in front of the candle.
6. You can add your incense or essential oils diffuser to the altar if you want. They can also be added later when you're ready to perform a ritual.

Once you've finished putting everything in place, you're done! That's all you need to do to have your very own Kemetic altar.

Easy Hieroglyphic Spell

Hieroglyphs possess innate magical properties that allow you to create spells from them. A simple hieroglyph spell you can try is known as the "Good Fortune Spell." The hieroglyphs will look like this:

What it translates to is, "I give you good luck with Shai." Here's the breakdown of the individual words and their hieroglyphs:

1. = I (self)

The first hieroglyph is a man seated with his arms stretched outward. It represents the pronouns "I/me/my."

2. = Give

The second hieroglyph depicts a smaller triangle inside a larger triangle. It represents the verb "to give."

3. = You (singular)

The third and fourth hieroglyphs are a tethering rope and a quail chick. They combine to form the singular pronoun "you."

4. = Good luck

The fifth hieroglyph is a cartouche. It represents "good luck."

5. = With

The sixth and seventh hieroglyphs are a sieve and a human mouth. When the sieve is stacked on top of the mouth, it represents the preposition "with."

6.   𓇅𓄿𓇋𓇋𓀭   = Shai (god)

The eighth, ninth, tenth, and eleventh hieroglyphs are a pool with lotus flowers, an Egyptian vulture, double reed panicles, and a seated man with a headdress and a postiche (false beard). They combine to form the name "Shai." He is the god of fate, and he is often associated with luck and fortune.

Chapter 3: The Neteru: Kemetic Deities and Their Stories

The Neteru are the prime gods of the Ancient Egyptian pantheon. For over 3,000 years, they were worshipped by the followers of the Ancient Egyptian religion. Even after their belief system was made illegal by the pagan-fearing Christians in the sixth century, their religion survived by going underground. Without a unifying authority like the pharaoh, the Ancient Egyptian religion fragmented, resulting in numerous sects that each had its own high priest or other religious leaders. This made it easier for Christianity to sweep through the region and convert large swathes of locals to the newer religion.

Despite the rise of Christianity and Islam in Egypt, the Ancient Egyptian religion was kept alive. No matter how hard the Roman Empire and its successors tried, they never managed to snuff it out completely. Kemetism is directly linked to the original Ancient Egyptian religion through the sects that carried on their traditions in secret. The Neteru developed out of these sects as well, when certain iterations of the Ancient Egyptian coalesced into the forms in use today. Modern Kemetism still recognizes the thousands of deities within the pantheon, but the Neteru have risen to become the prime gods of the religion.

The Neteru and Divine Symbolism

Unlike the pantheons of other pagan and neopagan religions, the Neteru are considered more than just gods. They are manifestations of natural forces, cosmic principles, and the laws of the universe. The Neteru also embody the spiritual beliefs and traditions of Kemetism itself. Symbolically, they represent a variety of ideas, aspects, and forces that weave through our lives. Whether or not you realize it, you encounter them every single day.

Without the Neteru, the universe would grind to a halt, and all of existence would come crashing down. We depend on them to keep the world spinning and the stars burning. The Neteru aren't haughty deities who look down on the mortal realm and interfere with people's lives like the gods of some other pagan pantheons - their reach extends from the smallest grain of sand to the vastest galaxy and beyond. Every one of those concepts encapsulates the divine symbolism of the Neteru.

Natural Forces

All of the Neteru are associated with at least one natural force. Their connection to nature is unrivaled since they exist in every aspect of the natural world. The rushing waters of the Nile River, the lions hunting the antelope, and the sun baking the desert sands are all imbued with the power of the Neteru. The elements of fire, water, earth, and air each have a corresponding god. There is a god of vegetation that grows and brims with life, a god that makes volcanoes erupt, and a god that controls the weather across the world. Every flower, tree, lake, river, insect, and animal has a god responsible for their existence.

Top of Murchison Falls Rapids on River Nile in Uganda.[33]

African Lions in Hunting.[53]

Volcano Eruption Next to Litli-Hrútur in Iceland in 2023.[54]

Cosmic Principles and Universal Laws

Cosmic principles and the laws of the universe are expressed through the Neteru by the individual gods' connection to them. There is a god of creation, a god of order, a god of chaos, and a god of entropy. Ma'at represents balance, and Heka represents magic. The gods are personifications of these concepts, and they can be viewed as primordial aspects in addition to being avatars of those ideas. Ma'at is the goddess of balance, but all expressions of balance in the universe are also "maat." There is no separation between the Neteru and the cosmic principles or universal laws.

Universal Energy

The universe remains in motion thanks to the universal energy created by the endless cycle of life. When a tree dies, but one of its acorns starts to grow, or when a star goes supernova and destroys everything in its path, but a new star ignites in the aftermath, it generates universal energy. The Neteru are responsible for the resurrection of souls in the afterlife, and those in control of the changing seasons create universal energy with every cycle of death and rebirth. That energy powers the cosmic and natural forces, spending it to propel life forward so it can continue rolling into the cycle of destruction and renewal.

The Neteru Creation Myths

Diving deeper into the Neteru creation myths, we can investigate the origins of Ptah, the Ennead, and the Ogdoad. These are the foundational stories on which the Kemetic belief system is based. These myths can be taken at face value and interpreted literally, but the vivid imagery and clever allegories help to paint a picture of how people should live their lives. You can interact with the world in a way that relates to the lessons imparted by the Neteru creation myths and discover the secret to bringing your life into balance.

Ptah Myth

Before the creation of the universe, the chaotic primordial waters of Nu existed. Ptah swam through the depths of Nu for untold eons. One day, he conceived the idea of the universe. It began with vague notions and abstract ideas of a world teeming with activity. As the concepts solidified in his mind, Ptah began to speak. From his mouth spilled the words of creation. He gave form to his thoughts and ideas. The first traces of the universe were built up from nothingness.

Ptah became more enthusiastic, shouting out names and commands to shape the universe around him. He told the mountains to rise up from the earth and ordered the rivers to zigzag across the land. His words brought the other gods into being, and when he uttered the names of the

The Creator God Ptah-Tatenen-Osiris.[35]

plants and animals, each one came to life. Finally, he conjured humanity into existence with little more than a flick of his tongue. All the stars and planets poured out of his heart, filling the cosmos with a whirlwind of activity.

The Ptah creation myth positions him as the chief of the Neteru, almost akin to the God and Creator of monotheistic religions. He was the patron god of Memphis, and when the city became the capital of Egypt during the First Dynasty, he was given prominence over the other Neteru. The Greeks equated Ptah with Hephaestus, and the Romans followed suit, identifying him as Vulcan. As part of the syncretic traditions of Kemetism, Ptah can be merged with other gods, such as Osiris and Tatenen, to create a deity with dominion over more aspects of the world.

Although other versions of the creation myth keep Ptah on the same level as the other Neteru, he is always involved in the creation of the universe in some manner. His creation myth is an expression of the power of language and the mind. Ptah forged the universe with nothing more than his intellect and oration skills. We can use these same skills in our own lives, sharing ideas and facilitating communication to help build something new.

Ennead Myth

The Ennead creation myth elevates Atum to the role of chief god and creator of the universe but in a different way than the Ptah myth. It starts with the benben rising from the chaotic waters of Nu, creating the first mound of firm stone. Atum emerged from the depths of the waters and climbed atop the benben. Here, he was merged with Ra to become Atum-Ra. He either spit, sneezed, or masturbated, resulting in the creation of the god Shu and the goddess Tefnut, who embodied air and moisture, respectively. Now that there were three deities, they were able to divide the responsibilities of creation.

Reconstructed Pyramidion of the Gaza Plateau Pyramids Representing the Benben.[86]

Shu and Tefnut mated and birthed two more gods: Geb and Nut. Geb was the personification of the earth, and Nut represented the night sky. They had four children together: Osiris, Isis, Set, and Nephthys. Osiris was the god of fertility, and he coupled with Isis, the goddess of order. Set and Nephthys paired off as well. He was the god of chaos, and she was the goddess of death, serving as a counterbalance to Osiris and Isis. The nine gods of the Ennead set about to create the aspects of the universe that they represented.

Atum-Ra ignited the sun in the sky, taking it along a path across the sky; Geb shaped the mountains, hills, and valleys; Nut brought about the constellations and the moon to fill the sky when the sun disappeared; Osiris sowed seeds into the soil to bring life to the earth; Isis formed the cycles of life, where all living things are born, grow, decay, die, and are reborn; Set brought forth opposing forces that could interrupt the life cycle or cut it short; and Nephthys established the realm of the dead, where the souls of the departed would end up.

The Ennead creation myth has Atum-Ra grow a family tree by way of parthenogenesis, where his offspring were born without the need for sexual reproduction. The rest of the Ennead are born through traditional means, but as is the case with the Greek and Roman gods, each couple is both a pair of siblings and a pair of mates. However, there are no incestual overtones in the myth; this is due to the inborn trait of shifting aspects within each god. When they need to be siblings, they present themselves as brothers and sisters, but when they take on the role of mates, they do so without the aspects of themselves that are biologically related.

There is more of an emphasis on the sun in the Ennead creation myth. Its connection to Atum-Ra gives it additional properties as a source of life, letting its warm rays nourish the world below. Even though the gods of the Ennead are given nearly equal status, there is still a hierarchy laid out by their family tree. Atum-Ra is always on top, just like the sun is always above the earth. But the sun disappears during the night, allowing the other gods a chance to take precedence in the pantheon. This reflected the political state of Egypt at the time; the pharaoh was the leader of the kingdom, but when he wasn't exercising his authority, local and regional leaders were given authority over their domains.

Ogdoad Myth

In the Ogdoad creation myth, Nu is depicted as personifying the chaotic primordial waters that precede the creation of the universe. All eight gods of the Ogdoad dwelled in the waters and took on aspects of them. Nu and his counterpart, Naunet, represented the actual waters in which they lived. Huh and Hauhet would swim across the limitless waters, testing the bounds of infinity. Kek and Kauket dove into the inky black depths, where the darkness gave way to the void. Amun and Amaunet kept the secrets hidden within the currents, never staying in one place.

An unexpected cataclysm caused the benben to rise from the waters. On the benben was a lotus flower, from which the sun bloomed. It shined brightly and bathed the waters in light. This stirred something within the Ogdoad, and they converged on the benben to discover the origins of the light. When they looked upon the sun, it filled their minds with dreams of new creations. The benben expanded into a great canvas made of earth onto which they could bring their dreams to life.

Nu and Naunet emerged from the primordial waters first. They created the rivers, lakes, and seas, carrying the waters across the world. Huh and Hauhet made the limitless skies, allowing the sun to rise into the heavens above. Amun set the sun in motion across the sky, and Amaunet created the underworld so it could rest before starting the journey anew. Kek formed the shade and shadows that stayed cool during the day, and Kauket threw a veil over the skies while it was gone, giving the gift of night.

The Ogdoad.⁹⁷

Once the world was made, the Ogdoad set about to populate it. Nu and Naunet brought forth all aquatic creatures, including the frogs and snakes that live around the waterbanks. Huh and Hauhet created birds, bats, and flying insects that could enjoy the skies. Kek and Kauket forged the animals that lived underground, in caves and holes, and those that only came out at night. Amun and Amaunet made the flora and fauna that thrived in the day, including the earliest humans. From all members of the Ogdoad came the other gods, such as Osiris, Isis, and Set.

The Ogdoad creation myth doesn't ascribe the majority of creation to a single god; instead, it treats the Ogdoad as entirely equal in importance. The omission of Ra as a creator god was likely due to power struggles that occurred between the times of the Middle and New Kingdoms. The centralized power of the 12th Dynasty was splintered in the wake of Queen Sobekneferu's death, and the city-states of Egypt began to vie for control. The region was also invaded and conquered by the Hyksos, who worshipped foreign gods. This destabilized the popularity of certain deities and pushed the various patron gods to the forefront.

By the time the Ogdoad myth first appeared early in the New Kingdom, Ra had been absorbed by several other gods, including Atum, Khepri, Khnum, and Montu. When Thebes was once again made Egypt's capital city during the New Kingdom, their patron god, Amun, gained more prominence across the kingdom. They even claimed Thebes as the location where the benben first appeared. After Amun was merged with Ra to become Amun-Ra, he took on extra importance in later versions of the Ogdoad creation myth.

The Prime Neteru

The prime Neteru are the eleven gods that hold the most power in the Egyptian pantheon.

Ra

Hieroglyphic Name:

Symbol: Sun Disk
Color: Gold
Element: Fire

Ra is the god of the sun, sky, order, and kings. He is usually depicted with the head of a falcon or ram and wearing a sun disk set within a headdress in the shape of the uraeus. The myths about Ra include his journey to carry the sun across the sky. He made the journey in a solar *barque* (a type of boat) called the *Mandjet*, and wore his falcon head during the voyage. Once he reached the uttermost west, he switched to a lunar barque called the *Mesektet*, and swapped to his ram head. Ra then had to sail across the underworld in order to reach the uttermost east, where he switched back to the Mandjet and his falcon head at dawn to begin the journey again.

The Sun God Ra.[38]

You can connect to the sun god Ra by performing rituals around large flames, like a campfire or bonfire. Offerings include flowers like marigolds, daylilies, wild oxeye daisies, sunflowers, or morning glories; food and drinks like orange juice, grapes, raisins, dried dates, apricots, beer, figs, or flatbread; and incense or essential oils like frankincense, myrrh, or sage. Using items with a sun theme will help to get his attention, and the best time to connect with him is during the summer, when the days are at their longest, meaning he is in the sky for more hours.

Osiris

Hieroglyphic Name:

Symbol: Crook and Flail
Color: Green
Element: Fire

Osiris is the god of the dead, afterlife, resurrection, fertility, agriculture, and flora. He is usually depicted with green skin, representing his resurrection after being killed by his brother Set. His wife, Isis, used magic to restore him to life, but death would forever remain a part of his being. Osiris is the ruler of the underworld and gives the final judgment on the fate of a soul. However, he is also a bringer of life, embodying the duality present in many aspects of the world.

If you want to connect with Osiris, the first thing to remember is that you should never use sand or anything sand-related in your rituals, since sand is associated with Set. Offerings can be flowers like baby's breath, Easter lilies, or blue lotuses; food and drinks like chocolate, caramel, mead, limes, milk, or red meat; and incense or essential oils like jasmine, lavender, sandalwood, or vanilla. Include mirrors, seashells, mechanical clocks, or bells and chimes to help get his attention. The best time of year for rituals dedicated to Osiris is in the spring or autumn, when crops are planted or harvested, and the seasons are between summer and winter.

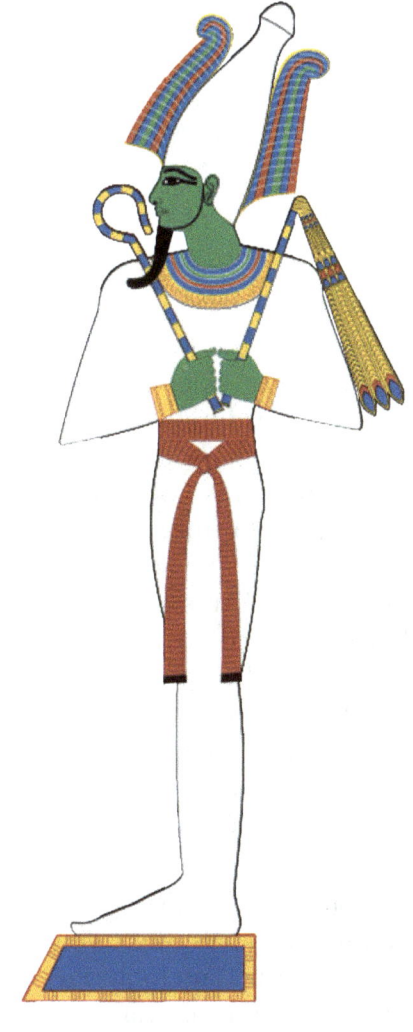

Osiris.[89]

Isis

Hieroglyphic Name:

Symbol: Tyet (Girdle of Isis)
Color: White
Element: Magic

Isis is the goddess of magic, fate, and the afterlife. She is often depicted wearing a headdress in the shape of the throne hieroglyph, a kite, or a sun disk with cow horns. She has a stronger connection to magic than any other deity, and she uses her powerful magic to resurrect her slain husband, Osiris. Isis is believed to help souls crossing over from the physical world to the afterlife, guiding them to the domain of her husband. There was a long-held tradition in Ancient Egypt that the pharaoh was symbolically the child of Isis.

You can connect with her by performing rituals where you circle your altar, clean up any footprints, and wear white ceremonial garb. Isis prefers offerings of flowers like lilies, irises, gardenias, or sweetpeas; food and drinks like milk, sweet wine, beer, bread, honey, cashews, or almonds; and incense or essential oils like rose, sandalwood, lavender, frankincense, myrrh, gum arabic, or lotus. She is a weaver, so using items of linen cloth can help to reach out to her. Using chants or hymns can also aid in gaining her blessings. The best time to contact Isis is during twilight or around 3 to 4 AM - when magic is said to be at its most potent.

Isis.[40]

Horus

Hieroglyphic Name:

Symbol: Eye of Horus
Color: Blue
Element: Air

Horus is the god of protection, healing, kingship, the sun, and the sky. He is the son of Osiris and Isis, from whom he inherited his position as one of the chief deities. Most common depictions of Horus include a falcon head, a pschent (a double crown of red and white), and holding a was-scepter and ankh. The conflict between Horus and his uncle Set is a major part of Ancient Egyptian mythology. During one of their battles, Set gouged out Horus' eye, although his mother was able to use magic to heal it. Horus eventually prevailed over his uncle, claiming his father's old throne and becoming a protector of Egypt.

Connecting with Horus requires you to enter a meditative state when performing rituals. Meditating will calm your soul and quiet your mind, allowing you to better reach out to him. Ancient Egyptians celebrated him annually during the Festival of Victory, so making offerings that include iron weapons or other war-related items will draw Horus to you. He likes food and drinks like beef, poultry, fruit, honey, beer, bread, and candied dates. You can also use incense or essential oils like frankincense, saffron, sandalwood, Egyptian musk, moringa oil, or acacia oil.

Horus.[41]

Anubis

Hieroglyphic Name:

Symbol: Jackal
Color: Black
Element: Earth

Anubis.

Anubis is the god of the Duat, funerary rites, mummification, embalming, and secrets. He serves as a guide to the underworld, a protector of graves, and the messenger of the gods. Most depictions of Anubis show him with the head of a jackal, and he's said to be the attendant of the scale during the Weighing of the Heart ritual. His parentage is complicated, as while his mother is always said to be Nephthys, the identity of his father is disputed between Set, Osiris, and Ra.

You can forge a connection with Anubis by invoking his name and role as a psychopomp. Offerings include flowers like black roses, blue lotuses, or lilies; food and drinks like dark-roasted coffee, cheese, red meat, dark liquor, blackberries, or sourdough; and incense or essential oils like frankincense, myrrh, vanilla, cloves, cinnamon, or pumpkin spice. Items like bones, feathers, puzzle boxes, bandages, antique keys, or scales can also help to earn his favor. Make sure you are always respectful of Anubis and treat him with the dignity he deserves.

Hathor

Hieroglyphic Name:

Symbol: Cow
Color: Green
Element: Air

Hathor is the goddess of the sky, joy, fertility, beauty, childbirth, motherhood, music, and dance. She is closely associated with aurochs, also known as great wild cows, which were considered to be maternal and celestial animals by Ancient Egyptians. Hathor is Ra's daughter, serves as the Eye of Ra, and is Horus's consort. Ancient Egyptian society drew their conceptions of femininity from Hathor, and she has aspects that represent the different stages of life experienced by women. She is present at birth, during childhood, while falling in love and getting married, becoming a mother, growing old, and dying. After death, Hathor helps to lead their souls to the afterlife.

You can connect with Hathor by performing rituals that involve music and dancing. Wearing makeup, eyeliner, and other cosmetics can help

Hathor.[48]

to gain her attention. You can make offerings of flowers like orange carnations, roses, acacias, lotuses, or hibiscuses; food and drinks like milk, bread, oatmeal, or chocolate; and incense or essential oils like saffron, myrrh, or lilac. If you can involve a sistrum during your rituals, your chances of receiving Hathor's blessings would be much higher. Play up her association with beauty and femininity to bring forth her power.

Sekhmet

Hieroglyphic Name:

Symbol: Lioness
Color: Red
Element: Fire

Sekhmet is the goddess of fire, war, and medicine. Like Hathor, she is Ra's daughter and one of the Eyes of Ra. She is depicted as having the head of a lioness and wearing a sun disk in a uraeus-shaped headdress. Sekhmet is an expression of the duality within the human heart – she represents both violence and healing, as well as the endless cycle of life and death. Fire can be a bringer of life, or it can be a destroyer. Her consort is Ptah, and she is sometimes paired with her sister, the feline goddess Bastet.

You can make a connection with Sekhmet by invoking her role as a healer and requesting her blessings to help treat an illness or injury. You can also appeal to her martial side, calling on her power with a war chant. Try giving her offerings of flowers like witch hazel, red poppies, calla lilies, and tulips; food and drinks like red wine, chili peppers, pomegranates, or red meat; and incense or essential oils like cinnamon, dragon's blood, black salt, copal, or frankincense.

Sekhmet.⁴⁴

Thoth

Hieroglyphic Name:

Symbol: Ibis
Color: Silver
Element: Magic

Thoth is the god of the moon, knowledge, wisdom, science, writing, art, judgment, and magic. He is often shown with an ibis head, which is also a symbol of his godhood. As the scribe of the gods, Thoth is responsible for keeping records of all their activities. He is also credited with inventing Egyptian hieroglyphs and helping to spread knowledge to the people of Ancient Egypt. Not only was he the mate of Ma'at, but he was the arbiter of laws, making sure to keep society in balance.

Connecting to Thoth is best achieved at night, under the light of a full moon. Bring him offerings related to writing and knowledge, such as pens, pencils, quills, ink, notepads, books, paper (especially papyrus), or typewriters. He also likes offerings of food and drinks like fruit, yogurt, moon water, green tea, chocolate, or granola bars, and incense or essential oils like rosemary, sage, peppermint, or lemon balm.

Thoth."

Bastet

Hieroglyphic Name:

Symbol: Cat
Color: Yellow
Element: Fire

Bastet is the goddess of cats, warfare, music, fertility, joy, love, and perfume. She is also considered the protector of pregnant women. As a daughter of Ra, she is associated with the Eye of Ra, like her sisters Hathor and Sekhmet. Bastet is typically depicted with the head of a cat or lioness and carrying a sistrum in one hand and an aegis in the other. Owing to her influence, cats became a sacred animal in Ancient Egypt. They would be carefully embalmed and mummified when they died, and killing them outside of ritualistic sacrifices was considered a crime punishable by death.

If you want to connect with Bastet, the best thing to do is include a cat or feline-related items in your rituals. She likes perfume, catnip, fish, milk, jewelry, and raw poultry. You can play music and perform an interpretive dance to bring her to your sacred space. Her blessings are always useful, but her role as a protector of pregnant women makes her aid particularly important if you're currently with child. Rituals dedicated to Bastet involving gemstones with chatoyancy, or a "cat's eye" marking, are more potent.

Bastet."

Khepri

Hieroglyphic Name:

Symbol: Scarab
Color: Blue
Element: Water

Khepri is the god of the morning sun and transformation. He is usually depicted with a scarab head and holding a was-scepter and ankh. Khepri is intrinsically linked to the sun god Ra, and some myths place him as being responsible for pushing the solar barque when its journey begins at dawn. Through his association with the scarab beetle, which Ancient Egyptians revered for its transformative properties, he is viewed as being related to renewal and rebirth. Many funerary objects like amulets and canopic jars bore the image of the scarab to help departed souls as they made their transition to the afterlife.

You can connect with Khepri by performing rituals at dawn. Recite a prayer to him when you spot the first light of the rising sun. Decorate your altar with scarabs and wear scarab-shaped jewelry. Offerings include morning glories, blue lotus flowers, turquoise, sunstones, thrush eggs, or beetle shells. You will have an easier time calling attention to yourself if you include words of praise and honor to Khepri at the same time as Ra and Atum, as they are considered three aspects of the sun: Khepri as the sunrise, Ra as the midday sun, and Atum as the sunset.

Khepri.[47]

Ptah

Hieroglyphic Name:

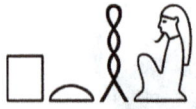

Symbol: Djed Pillar
Color: Green
Element: Water

In addition to his role as a creator deity, Ptah is the god of craftsmen, metalworking, painting, sculpting, carpentry, stonemasonry, and architecture. He is responsible for sudden bursts of inspiration and creativity, visualization of ideas and plans, and blessing crafting tools to ensure the success of a project. Even ancient Egyptian traditions that didn't believe Ptah to be the creator of the world acknowledged his feat of self-creation, as he has never attested to having parents. His consort is either Sekhmet or Bastet.

You can connect with Ptah by involving something related to arts and crafts in your rituals. Offerings include food and drinks like bread, fish, wine, stew, barley, or fruit; items like crafting tools, clay, precious metals, gemstones, or works of art; and incense or essential oils like frankincense, jasmine, rosemary, lavender, eucalyptus, tea tree oil, or cedarwood. Decorate your altar with green or blue cloth, clay offering vessels, a potter's wheel, or the symbols of the ankh, djed pillar, and was-scepter.

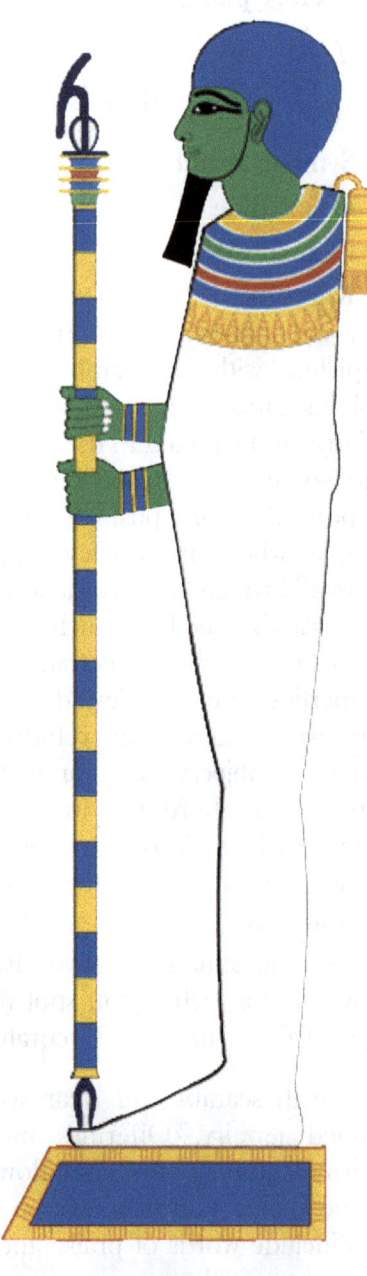

Ptah.[48]

Bonding with the Neteru

Creating a bond with the Neteru is essential if you're serious about your dedication to Kemetism. A practitioner without a connection to the gods would be like a painter without a brush, canvas, or color palette. Meditation can help you focus on making contact with the Neteru by banishing any distractions from your mind. Reciting prayers, singing hymns, and chanting spells dedicated to one or all of the Neteru is a great way to more fully feel their presence and power. Performing rituals and making appropriate offerings will catch their attention and establish a link between you and them.

As you become more immersed in Kemetism, you'll start to see signs that the Neteru are all around you. A lightning storm might indicate that Set is near, while Sekhmet might cause a spontaneous fire. When you hear beautiful music or joyous laughter, you can be sure that Hathor or Bastet is close by. A clear day in the middle of July is the perfect time for Ra to make an appearance. Once you start paying attention to the details around you, you'll begin to notice just how often these signs will appear. The Neteru are everywhere since they're not only gods but the forces that bind the universe together.

Practical Exercises

Getting to know the Neteru is exciting, but you should take some time to reflect on their role in the world and in your life. Here are some exercises you can do to bring you closer to the Neteru and announce your intention to connect with them:

Neteru Offering Ritual

The purpose of this ritual is to seek the blessings of the Neteru and maintain the cosmic balance. Perform it around dawn or dusk for the best results.

Here's what you'll need:

- Altar or sacred space
- Candle
- White cloth
- Bowl of clean water
- Frankincense or myrrh incense

- An offering of bread, honey, wine, flowers, or fruit
- A short invocation prayer

Once you have everything collected, follow these steps to perform the ritual:

1. Wash your face and hands in the bowl of water to purify yourself.
2. Place the white cloth over your altar or on the ground of your sacred space.
3. Arrange your offering on the cloth.
4. Light the candle and incense.
5. If it's dawn, face east, and if it's dusk, face west, then recite your invocation prayer:

    Oh great Neteru!

    I come before you with reverence in my heart and honor in my soul,

    To humbly make this offering.

    Allow it to sustain you, as you sustain our world.

    Take this [offering name] as a token of my gratitude,

    Enjoy this gift as I enjoy the fruits of your divine labor.

    Praise be to the Neteru!

6. Sit or kneel and meditate in silence for several minutes. Reflect on the Neteru and the balance of the world.
7. When you finish meditating, say, "Thank you, great Neteru, for your presence and blessings. I shall strive to uphold maat in all that I do."
8. Leave the offering for the Neteru until the candle or incense burns out. You can either consume or dispose of the offering afterward.

Neteru Invocations

You can practice your invocations to the Neteru so that you're able to recite them from memory during your rituals. Start with this invocation to Ra:

Oh great Ra!

God of the Sun, Bringer of Light, and Lord of Both Horizons,

I call upon your mighty powers to grant me clarity in purpose,

Strength of will and fires of passion to sustain me during my trials.

I offer you my boundless devotion,
Singing your praises as the eastern sun rises,
And heralding your rebirth as the western sun dies.
Oh great Ra!
I honor your name and worship your light,
May its burning glory shine on me evermore.
Cleanse me in your heat; purify me with your fire,
And never let the darkness overtake my heart.
Praise be to Ra!

Here's an invocation dedicated to Isis:

Oh great Isis!
Divine Mother, Lady of Joy, and Mistress of Magic,
I ask that you guide me in my moment of need.
Help me find my way to the truth,
And keep my heart and mind in balance.
My mind unravels from elusive thoughts.
Like the threads of fate woven through my soul,
Guide me through the perils that surround me.
I am lost, Mother Isis – show me the path home.
I give thanks for your wisdom,
And offer up my grateful heart.
You, the Mistress of the Beautiful West,
Shall endure long after my bones turn to dust.
Praise be to Isis!

Finally, try out this invocation to Osiris:

Oh great Osiris!
God of the Dead, Prince of Eternity, and He Who Rises Again,
Though once you were slain, you live yet again.
The Judge of Souls and King of the Blessed Dead,
I call to you from the world of the living.
My heart craves justice, but my soul pleads for mercy,
Whisper to me words of comfort from the Land of the Dead.

Give me a sign that the wicked can't escape your notice,
And that true judgment is pronounced from your lips.
Accept my words as one who seeks balance,
Who wishes to make right what once went wrong.
Help me endure this pain and keep my back unbroken,
So I can fulfill my promise to live a good life.
I shall walk in your footsteps as I follow your lead,
And honor you to the end of my days.
When the time comes to cast off my final breath,
I shall meet you on the banks of the Nile as a friend.
Praise be to Osiris!

Chapter 4: The Power of Heka

Heka is the mystical energy that surrounds the universe and binds us all together. It was a fundamental force that existed at the start of creation, and it helps to sustain the entire universe. Those with the knowledge and skill to tap into the power of heka can manipulate reality, create things out of nothing, and even return the dead to life. Gods and humans alike have the potential to tap into heka and use it. Those who wish to wield this magic can do so through rituals, spells, prayers, incantations, and magical objects like amulets and charms. With the power of heka at your fingertips, there are no limits to what you can achieve.

Statue of Heka.[40]

Heka and Ancient Egyptian Society

According to the Ancient Egyptian pharaoh Merikare, heka was a gift bestowed upon humanity from the creator gods. It was meant to enhance the experience of living a mortal life in the physical realm, giving people a small taste of the divine. Having the ability to control the elements, heal the sick and wounded, and nudge the strands of fate would allow humans a chance to briefly feel what it's like to be a god. While magic was accessible by anyone, Ancient Egyptian society developed a hierarchy when it came to who was permitted knowledge of specific rituals or spells, as well as who was allowed to perform certain types of magic.

At the top of the hierarchy was the pharaoh. The pharaoh was considered a living incarnation of the gods, so his direct link to the pantheon put him above everyone else. There weren't any restrictions on what magic the pharaoh could perform, and they had access to the vast wealth of magical knowledge in the royal libraries and temple archives. Right below the pharaoh was the priesthood, which had its own levels of rank that conferred more privileges the higher up the ladder a priest climbed. After the lowest-ranking priests was the laity. That consisted of all other citizens who lived within the kingdom. They had the most restrictions on the practice of magic, but they were still able to engage with heka and the gods on a regular basis.

Restrictions on Magic

The Ancient Egyptians revered heka as a force that could enact significant change to the natural course of events, making it a power not to be used lightly. They believed that their rituals, spells, and invocations had a tangible effect on people and the world around them, which meant there existed the potential for abuse. The priesthood viewed certain aspects of magic as a weapon that could be wielded against enemies, so there was an inherent danger to unregulated practice by the masses. Their solution was to clearly delineate what magic the laity was legally able to use.

Restricting access to magic was often presented as being for religious reasons, such as claiming that it was offensive to the gods for a regular citizen to perform a ritual classified for high-ranking priests or members of the royal family. However, the reality was that these restrictions were politically motivated. The upper echelon of Ancient Egyptian society feared the power that could be wielded by regular citizens if they were given free access to the totality of their civilization's magical knowledge.

The potential for mass uprisings would put the current leadership in a very precarious position.

Part of what helped keep the people in line and the ruling class in power was their exclusive right to restricted magic. If the kingdom experienced a crisis like a famine, the pharaoh and priesthood were the only ones who could legally perform rituals to lift it. While a lack of success could put them in danger of usurpation by those in the line of succession, their failures could usually be explained away. But if that magic was available to everyone, any random citizen could try their hand at the ritual. Should a simple farmer succeed where the pharaoh and priesthood failed, it would completely undermine the people's faith in the ruling class.

Once their faith was shattered, the people would have no reason to continue following those in power. The masses could rally behind that farmer, overthrow the current leaders, and elevate him to the throne. That lack of stability and trust in the ruling class could easily become an endless cycle of rebellions every time a problem befell the kingdom. Without a fixed line of succession and class division, local uprisings following different leaders would inevitably clash, and the kingdom would lose all sense of unity. Instead of a strong central power in the form of the pharaoh, Egypt would've fragmented into a collection of warring petty kingdoms, not unlike the state of England prior to the Norman Conquest.

The Priesthood

The priesthood of Ancient Egypt was divided into hierarchies of both rank and duty. There were great sanctuaries in most major cities, usually dedicated to the local patron god. The pharaoh appointed the leaders of each great sanctuary, who had a cadre of priests and clerics serving them. Each member of the priesthood was appointed by their peers and senior officials, which often resulted in politicking and backroom deals as the priests jockeyed for better positions.

The high priests who served as the leaders of the great sanctuaries didn't have a uniform title. Instead, each temple had its own title, and many were also assigned an official epithet. The epithets were usually related to the patron god of the cities where the great sanctuary was located. They included:

- **Heliopolis:** The High Priest of Ra was called the "Greatest of Seers." This referenced how Ra could see across vast distances with his falcon eyes while journeying through the sky.

- **Memphis:** The High Priest of Ptah was called the "Chief of the Artisans" or the "Greatest of the Directors of Craftsmanship." This referenced Ptah's role as the god of craftsmen and artisans.
- **Thebes (Karnak):** The High Priest of Amun was called the "Chief Prophet of Amun" or the "First Prophet of Amun," and had the epithet "The One Who Opens the Two Gates of Heaven." The two Gates of Heaven were the eastern and western horizons, which were considered gateways through which the sun and moon traveled daily.
- **Hermopolis:** The High Priest of Thoth was called the "Great One of the Five." The "Five" in the title referred to Thoth and four other gods: Nu, Heh, Kek, and Amun.
- **Abydos:** The High Priest of Osiris lacked any other titles or epithets. However, the high priest who served in that role during the reign of Ramesses II was named Wenennefer, which means "The One Who Continues to Be Perfect," and was one of Osiris' epithets.

Below the high priests were the other senior priests, some of whom had titles of their own, like the Second, Third, and Fourth Prophets of Amun. The majority of the priests at any given temple were from the lower ranks and often worked as temple servants. They were assigned specific roles to ensure the temple always had priests who could perform the necessary tasks and duties. These included:

- **Lector Priests:** They received extensive training in the sacred texts and spells so they could recite prayers and incantations during important festivals and ceremonies.
- **Sem Priests:** They were experts in burial practices and funerary rites and were charged with performing mummification rituals and casting spells to help guide the departed souls through their trials in the afterlife.
- **Wab Priests:** Also known as "pure ones," they were the lowest ranking priests, responsible for keeping the temples clean and maintained, as well as assisting the higher ranking priests in their rituals and other duties.

The Laity

The laity of Ancient Egypt included every citizen who wasn't part of the priesthood or ruling class. These were the regular people who made up the bulk of the kingdom. They had significant limitations on the magic they could perform, and the knowledge they had access to was controlled by their local temples. However, the literacy rate of Ancient Egypt was only between 1 and 5%, with those capable of reading and writing mostly confined to scribes, high-ranking officials, and priests. For everyone else, the collections of sacred texts were useless, and they learned their heka rituals, spells, and incantations from their elders and priests.

Heka and the Divine

Heka is very closely associated with the divine forces of the universe. It's why Egyptologists have long struggled to agree on the exact conditions that classify a text, spell, or incantation as "magic" versus "religious." Many Ancient Egyptian rituals have the hallmarks of religious practices, yet their goals are often based in magic. Part of the problem stems from the biases of modern cultures, particularly in the West. Analyzing the beliefs of long-dead civilizations is usually looked at with a more critical and academic eye, whereas those same parameters are not applied to their own society's major religions.

Nobody would challenge the classification of the Bible as religious, but an objective reading would lead to the conclusion that many of the acts and events described in it are of a magical nature. Jesus transmogrified water into wine, Moses' brother Aaron transformed an inanimate rod into a living snake, and Elijah's ritual called fire down from Heaven. If you replaced the Biblical characters with a wizard, everyone would agree that these were acts of magic. While Ancient Egyptians *did* believe in the existence of magic, without the benefit of contemporary context, it's difficult to know what they would have deemed magic versus religious – or even if they would make a distinction at all.

Heka and Creation

The creation of the universe never would have happened without heka. The actions taken by the creator gods in every version of the creation myth tapped into the power of heka to bring people, places, and things into existence. From the evidence currently available, it appears that Ancient Egyptians weren't as preoccupied with having an explanation for every part of a story as today's audiences. How did Atum have the ability to spawn Shu and Tefnut from his bodily fluids? Where did the benben come from if there was nothing but a sea of chaotic, primordial water? For that matter, who created that water and the deities that dwelled within it? The simple answer to all these questions is: heka.

Heka serves an important function in the creation myths, even if it's mostly confined to subtext. Magic allowed Atum to create Shu and Tefnut. So why did he never repeat that feat? Because of maat; because of the divine balance. Heka gave him the power to create two new gods since the universe needed additional gods to function. Once that was achieved, all further additions to the pantheon came from the mating of pairs. As there was no reason for Atum to retain the power of parthenogenesis, that specific manifestation of magic never reappeared. Heka was present and working behind the scenes the whole time. The primordial waters existed because heka existed. It raised the benben to kickstart the creation of the universe.

Heka and the Gods

Many of the gods' greatest feats were made possible through heka. Ptah's thoughts and words were brought into existence with magic. He was essentially casting the first spells – he made his intentions clear in his mind and spoke words of power to affect reality. Ra sails his solar barque across the sky to move the sun, thanks to heka. More obviously, Isis resurrected Osiris and healed Horus' eye through the explicit use of heka. It's the power behind the divinity of the gods. They would be no different from mortals without it.

Because of magic's mysterious nature, it takes a great deal of study and dedication to become adept in the subject. In Ancient Egypt, priests needed to be literate in order to read the sacred texts. Thoth exemplifies the correlation between intelligence and heka. He's the god of wisdom, knowledge, and magic, with many of his aspects being related to scholarly pursuits. He serves as the ideal that those practicing heka should strive to reach. You won't succeed in harnessing the power of heka if you aren't willing to put in the time and effort worthy of Thoth.

Hieroglyphic Spells

Most of the rituals, incantations, and spells from Ancient Egypt were recorded in the sacred texts with hieroglyphs. Magic was linked to them from the earliest days of Ancient Egyptian culture. Their name for the hieroglyphic writing system translates to "writing of the gods' words," which shows that they always viewed hieroglyphs as possessing an otherworldly power. That tradition continues to this day through Kemetism. The hieroglyphic spells used by Kemetic practitioners are rooted in the same beliefs that made the Ancient Egyptian sacred texts so powerful.

How It Works

Hieroglyphic spells use the inherent power of language and iconography to manifest magical results. Each individual hieroglyph represents a concept, force, or being. Most words and names used by modern languages are made up of multiple hieroglyphs. Each one conjures an aspect of the whole. Consider the following:

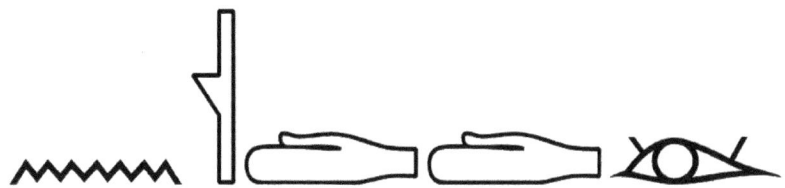

Taken on their own, they're just pictures of a water ripple, a stilt, two hands, and an eye touched up with paint. When read together, though, it suddenly becomes the word for "sleep." Each hieroglyph builds on the next, and while the reasons for certain choices of hieroglyphs might not make sense to us, it would've made perfect sense to Ancient Egyptians. Hieroglyphic spells work on a similar principle. Each hieroglyph chosen as part of the spell has a specific reason for being there, and they're all necessary for the spell to be successful.

Role of Scribes

Scribes in Ancient Egypt were among their society's most important professions. The ability to read their written language and be talented enough in the arts to create recognizable pictures was a rarity. They received a comprehensive education in reading, writing, and arithmetic, and the ruling class highly valued their services. Once a scribe earned a desirable position, they would raise their sons to follow in their footsteps and eventually inherit their role. They established unofficial lines of succession, not unlike the way pharaohs and high priests came to power.

Nearly all records were kept by scribes, who frequently transcended their original purpose of transcription and text reproduction. They were placed in charge of municipal planning and construction projects, given administrative and economic responsibilities, and entrusted with facilitating communication with foreign traders and officials. They also recorded stories from the lower classes that were primarily passed down orally, preserving them for posterity when they would have otherwise been long forgotten. Without those scribes and their hieroglyphs, much of our knowledge about Ancient Egypt wouldn't exist.

Kemetic Rituals

The rituals of Kemetism employ the power of heka to pay tribute to the gods and bring forth the desired effects. It should be noted that these rituals aren't about commanding magical forces to bend to your will - they're about asking for an outcome in exchange for offerings and exultations. The most powerful heka users have the greatest knowledge surrounding Kemetic rituals and have mastered the art of performing them. Knowing the best time for a ritual, what offerings appeal to each aspect of a given god, which invocations to recite, and the right way to address the deities are all important parts of ensuring a ritual's success.

Structure of a Ritual

While every specific ritual has its own cadence and unique facets, they all share a basic structure. When researching Kemetic rituals for different purposes and occasions, you can expect them to include the following:

- **Altar and/or Sacred Space**: Nearly all rituals require an altar dedicated to the gods or an area that has been cleansed and blessed. Making the necessary preparations is actually part of the ritual. It helps to prove your intentions for undertaking the ritual aren't impulsive or half-hearted. Anyone who can't be bothered to properly set up an altar or sacred space will have their ritual fail, no matter what they were trying to achieve.

- **Establishing Action**: This usually consists of lighting a candle to signal the official opening of the ritual. The fire of the flame represents the light of knowledge casting off the darkness of ignorance. A candle is also finite, like the lifespan of a mortal. It acknowledges that you understand your earthly existence is fleeting while the power of the gods is eternal.

- **Purification**: Most rituals call for you to wash yourself with blessed water or burn incense to purify your mind, body, and spirit. Each god has certain types of incense that appeals to them, and various fragrances grant different benefits or attributes. Scent is a powerful sensation often linked to memories and emotions. Bringing them to the surface allows you to be vulnerable and authentic, which is necessary for a ritual to succeed.

- **Item Offerings**: You can't ask the gods for assistance without giving something in return. Offerings are meant to make it clear how important the outcome of the ritual is to you. Showing your willingness to lose something of material or emotional value right now in exchange for the possibility of a greater reward in the future helps to prove your dedication.

- **Food Offerings**: The gods gain sustenance through food and drink offerings. Your choice of what to give them will tell them a lot about you. As you perform more of these rituals, you'll establish a rapport with the gods, and you'll be able to figure out which foods and drinks get the best results. Because of the personal nature of these relationships, it can vary from one person to the next.

- **Prayers, Incantations, or Invocations**: Reciting a prayer that gives thanks to the gods and calling attention to your offerings shows that you're grateful to them and aren't seeking their power for selfish reasons. Incantations prove your devotion to the beliefs of Kemetism, as well as the fact that you take the religion seriously enough to learn them. Invocations display your reverence of the gods and show that you have a healthy respect for the immensity of power they possess.

- **Meditation and Reflection**: You should always take the time to put aside all worldly distractions and focus on balancing your mind, body, and spirit. Meditation slows things down so you don't jump ahead of yourself in your eagerness to complete the ritual. You can reflect on the nature of the gods, heka, maat, and how the beliefs of Kemetism factor into your daily life.

- **Closing Action**: Ending a ritual without properly closing it out not only risks ruining all your hard work in preparing and performing it, but also leaves yourself open to the intrusion of ill-intentioned spirits. If you think of a ritual like inviting a guest over for a visit, forgetting to close it out would be like forgetting to lock your door after your guest leaves. While there's a chance you won't suffer any negative consequences, if something *does* manage to get in, it can cause considerable harm to you. Closing actions are simple gestures like blowing out the candle, bowing your head, and repeating an affirmation, so there's no reason to skip this part of the ritual.

Sacred Gestures

Sacred gestures like the Dua are depicted.[50]

Sacred gestures are a form of veneration that uses specific hand movements, postures, and poses that symbolize the gods, cosmic forces, and ancient traditions. You can use sacred gestures during rituals and prayers to help forge a stronger connection with the Neteru and the power of heka. Popular sacred gestures include:

- **Dua**: Based on the posture depicted in many hieroglyphs representing worship or praise. It consists of sitting or kneeling with both hands outstretched in front of you. This gesture shows that you acknowledge the power of the gods and are offering them your honor and respect.

- **Pose of Immortality**: A series of brief poses that synergize physical movement, breathing, and energy flow. It's based on a combination of Ancient Egyptian prayer rituals and spiritual yoga poses. You can perform it by following these steps:

1. Sit on your knees with your toes pointed behind you.
2. Lift your right knee to your chest and set your right foot flat on the ground.
3. Place your right elbow against the inside of your right thigh.
4. Twist your torso to the left while exhaling slowly. Keep your right elbow pressed to your thigh.
5. Bring your hands together in front of your chest as if saying a prayer.
6. Make a loose fist and open your right arm, followed by your left. Your right elbow should still be pressed against your thigh.
7. Turn your head to the right while letting out your breath.
8. Inhale and bring your head back to the middle.
9. Exhale and turn your head to the left.
10. Repeat steps 2 through 9 with your left knee to your chest and left elbow against your left thigh. Make sure to reverse the direction you move as well.

Postures of the Gods: Different postures you can adopt during rituals that mimic the poses used by popular depictions of the gods.

Pose of Selkhet:

Pose of Anubis:

Pose of Osiris:

Pose of Thoth:

Recitations and Chants

Many Kemetic rituals involve the recitation of prayers or chants. Reciting a prayer to the gods doesn't have to only happen during rituals or festivals. You can offer a prayer while exercising, folding laundry, or relaxing on the couch. Chants can also be performed outside of rituals, like to thank the gods before a meal or as a celebration after your favorite sports team wins the big game. Reciting prayers and chants in your free time helps to keep the gods present in your mind and shows that you're willing to honor them while going about your daily life.

Iconomancy

Iconomancy is a form of magic that uses icons representing deities to cast spells or complete rituals. Icons can be artistic interpretations of the gods, like paintings, carvings, or statues, or they can be sacred symbols used as a stand-in, usually an object or animal more closely associated with a particular god. For example, the sacred symbols of Isis include a moon disk, a kite, and a tyet knot, while a crescent moon, papyrus scroll, and ibis are sacred symbols of Thoth. When using iconomancy, you need to make sure you prepare the icons with a blessing. Otherwise, they won't act as anything more than a regular altarpiece.

Heka in Your Daily Life

Ancient Egyptians recognized that heka was a part of their daily life. They made room in their routine for rituals and recitations, as it was important to them that they didn't neglect their spiritual health. People in the modern world won't hesitate to go to the gym or challenge their minds regularly, but exercising their spirituality is usually reserved for formal religious services and celebrations. You can use heka when brewing a cup of green tea in the afternoon by offering a prayer to Hathor. You can use it before going to bed at night, performing a ritual for Nephthys, or writing out a hieroglyphic spell to help your sore muscles instead of scrolling mindlessly on your phone. Heka was a gift to the world at its inception, and it remains our enduring legacy.

Practical Exercises

You can start practicing heka rituals and recitations right away. You don't need a lot of expensive supplies or wait for specific environmental factors to appear. All you really have to do is give heka the respect it deserves and try out these exercises:

Personal Heka Invocation

Personal heka invocations are something you create yourself, using aspects of your own life and personality to construct a prayer calling on the power of the gods for individual objectives. The more work you put into customizing your invocation, the stronger your connection with the gods will be. However, you can use this personal heka invocation template to start you off on the right track:

Oh great [name of god(dess)]!

I call on you as the god(dess) of [aspect of godhood] to help me [describe what you want].

I have searched across [city, state, province, or country you live] for signs of your presence,

And I have seen your power in the [describe your favorite thing locally].

In the north, the cooling winds bring you this offering of [drink];

In the south, the hearty earth brings you this offering of [food];

In the east, the cleansing fire brings you the light of dawn;

In the west, the purifying waters bring you the rising moon.

[Name of god(dess)], please look favorably upon your humble servant,

For I have not the wisdom nor experience that you possess.

While these [your eye color] eyes are not worthy to gaze on your splendor,

I ask that you remember my gifts to you and [repeat what you want].

I give you thanks, great [name of god(dess)]!

Chanting Practice

You can practice the sacred chant of Hathor while meditating or doing yoga. Just memorize these words and start off by slowly chanting:

El!

Ka!

Leem!

Om!

Keep repeating those four words over and over, increasing the speed of your chant each time you complete a cycle. When you are chanting as fast as you can, raise your arms up to the sky in veneration of the gods. Finally, chant the words one last time and stop, pulling your arms down at the same moment you go quiet. If you're wondering what you were chanting, it's pretty simple:

El=Earth

Ka=Fire

Leem=Water

Om=Air

Spoken Manifestation Spell with Ptah's Creative Power

Spoken manifestation spells are meant to replicate the magic Ptah used in his creation myth, namely bringing things into existence through nothing but thoughts and words. Form your intention and hold it in your mind as you repeat the spell:

From the waters of Nu I come

I speak "earth" and have a place to set my feet

I speak "river" and have a place to soak my hands

I speak "fire" and have a way to warm my bones

I speak "wind" and have a way to cool my brow

From the waters of Nu I came

To the gates of the Duat I go

Chapter 5: Key Kemetic Rituals

Now that you have a pretty solid foundation for your knowledge about Kemetism, the Neteru, heka, and maat, you can get into the "how to" of actually performing Kemetic rituals. They're rooted in the traditions of Ancient Egypt but have been adapted to the realities of the modern world. Ancient Egyptian rituals were extensive undertakings that could take hours to complete. Kemetism has taken the underlying beliefs and distilled them to their essence in order to revamp the ritual structure while preserving their original purpose. Kemetic rituals allow you to harness their power for self-improvement, positive energy, spiritual enhancement, and personal protection.

Types of Kemetic Rituals

There are many different types of Kemetic rituals, and each has a specific purpose. Your intentions when performing a ritual must always be crystal clear, and you have to take care to give the gods their due. It's also essential that you remember the principle of maat, making sure your actions and objectives remain balanced. If you rush in and skip steps because you want to get results as soon as possible, your ritual will fail to give you what you want. Not only would it be a waste of the gods' time, but you'd be short-changing yourself the opportunity for real personal growth.

Devotional Ritual

These are short, simple rituals designed to be repeated each day. The goal of a devotional is to align your spirit closer and closer to your chosen patron god. They're more informal than other types of rituals and don't require much preparation to perform. All you need is a candle, an altar, a shrine, or a sacred space, and about five minutes of free time.

Hands pressed together in prayer.

Invocation Ritual

These rituals call upon the power of an individual deity to help you achieve a specific goal. The chosen god can also be summoned to ask them for more intensive assistance. Invocation rituals usually involve prayers, chants, offerings, or other recitations. Over time, performing these rituals will begin to transform your own inner spirit and synchronize with the archetypal principles your patron god represents.

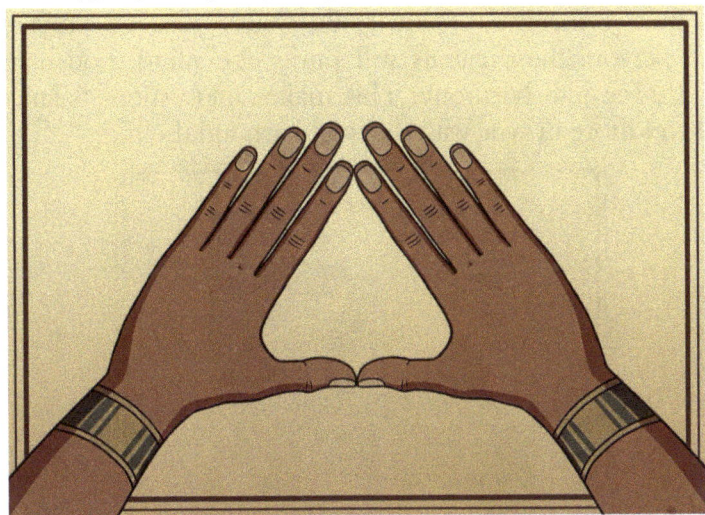
Hands using fingers and thumb to make a triangle.

Protection Ritual

These are performed primarily to protect yourself against various forms of harm. They can be to safeguard you from physical injuries, illnesses, diseases, stress, hopelessness, or mental anguish. Some protection rituals focus more on warding off ill-intentioned spirits, negative energy, or bad luck. There are a number of ways to approach a protection ritual, including using symbolic items, offerings, invocations, and prayers to the gods for their blessings.

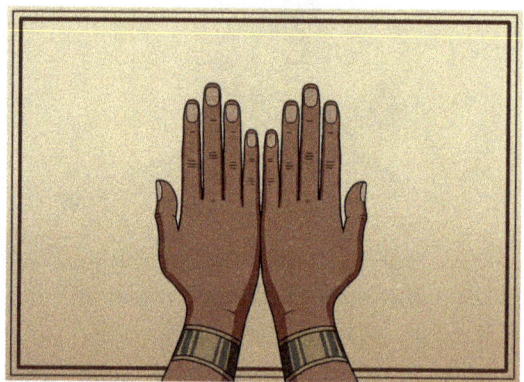

Hands held in front of face.

Cleansing Ritual

These allow you to cleanse a person, item, or space of negative energy, harmful spirits, and unseen corruption. Cleansing rituals are often performed as part of the preparation stage for a more extensive ritual. They can involve incense, essential oils, water, salt, and prayers. When used on a person, these rituals will purify the mind, body, and spirit, bringing all three into harmony. This makes them more balanced as an individual and more in sync with the world around them.

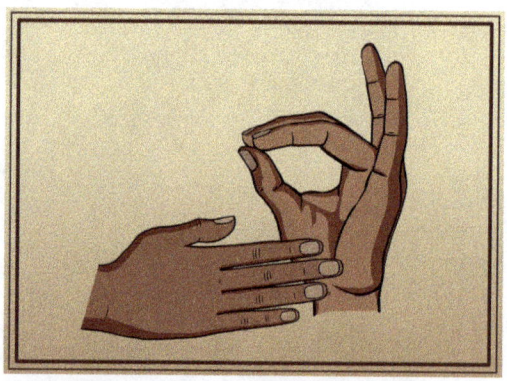

Hands making purification gesture of Hathor.

Healing Ritual

These rituals seek to identify, alleviate, and eliminate any physical, mental, emotional, or spiritual pain and suffering. They invoke the power of the gods, the elements, nature, or cosmic forces, bringing them to bear on the injuries or ailments the target for the ritual is experiencing. Healing rituals are often paired with traditional medical treatments, using heka to enhance secular healing techniques.

Hands held out with palms facing up.

Activation Ritual

These are rituals intended to activate the magic or spiritual energy locked inside a sacred object, such as an amulet, talisman, sigil, or idol. Activation rituals require you to imbue the object with an intention, which directs its power where it needs to go. These rituals can involve the four elements or cardinal directions, which have an inherent spiritual significance.

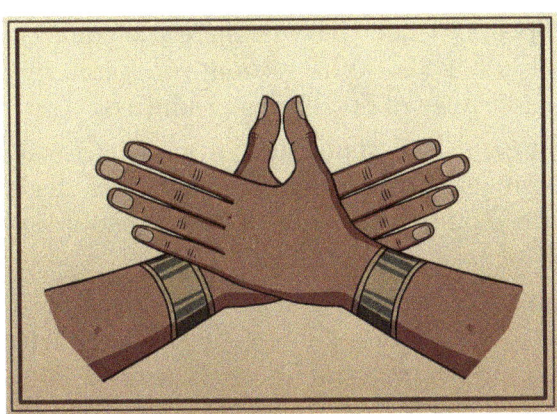

Hands making symbol of the phoenix.

Ritual Sequence

The sequence for a standard Kemetic ritual involves nine core steps, but there's always room for you to tailor each ritual to your own personality and style. Here's a quick rundown of the main parts of these rituals:

1. **Purification**: The purification rite of Kemetic rituals is adapted from the Ancient Egyptian ritual of Senut. You will cleanse yourself and your sacred space as a show of respect to the gods before engaging with them. Wash your hands and face or anoint the space with purified water. You can also use incense to purify the air around the space.

2. **Grounding**: Establish your sacred space. Lay a cloth down on the ground or over your altar. Place a candle in the middle. Arrange your offerings respectfully around the candle. If you have any icons of the gods, include them here.

3. **Opening Ceremony**: Light the candle and use it to perform an acknowledgment of the four cardinal directions. You can hold the candle or fold your hands together as you reach out toward each direction.

4. **Invocation**: Call upon the gods and invoke their power. Recite an invocation prayer and offer them praise. Depending on your intention, face in the cardinal direction associated with the god/power you're invoking.

5. **Offering**: Present the gods with your offering of food, drinks, flowers, incense, or sacred symbols. Lift each offering and ask for its acceptance.

6. **Prayer, Spell, or Chant**: This is where you connect with the divine power of the gods. What action you perform here tends to determine the type of ritual being conducted.

7. **Meditation and Reflection**: Take a moment to silently reflect on your communion with the gods and your feelings about the experience. You can meditate on your intention and if you uphold the ideals of maat.

8. **Reversion of Offering**: Ancient Egyptians were required to consume food or drink offerings before completing their rituals. Sharing in the offerings with the gods symbolized their acceptance and blessings. You'll do the same. Eat and drink what you can, and return what you can't to nature in an ethical manner.

9. **Closing Ceremony**: Thank the gods for their aid and bid them farewell. When you're done, blow out the candle and any burning incense. This signals that you're closing the sacred space, preventing any negative energy or harmful spirits from entering.

Private Kemetic altar.⁵¹

The Cardinal Directions

The cardinal directions are imbued with spiritual significance for practitioners of Kemetism. Each has its own symbols and representations that can guide your rituals or enhance the link between you and the gods. The point at the center of the four directions can serve as a nexus where the cardinal directions are connected and in complete balance.

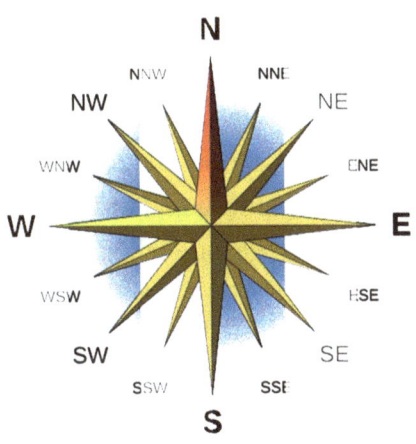
Compass Rose.⁵³

North

Associated with challenges, trials, endurance, willpower, winter, and darkness. Best used when you're experiencing hardships, being tested, acknowledging your limits, or in need of inner strength. Represents the darker aspects of Ma'at.

South

Associated with truth, justice, wisdom, order, summer, and light. Best used when seeking knowledge or guidance, overcoming obstacles, reflecting on personal growth, or achieving balance. Represents the lighter aspects of Ma'at.

East

Associated with birth, rebirth, life, new beginnings, endless possibilities, spring, and the sun. Best used when creating things, starting over, launching new endeavors, or looking forward to the future. Represents Osiris as the god of resurrection.

West

Associated with death, the afterlife, transformation, release, autumn, and the moon. Best used when ending relationships, working through emotions, undergoing a change, or trying to let go of something. Represents Osiris as the god of the dead.

Practical Exercises

With the knowledge of a Kemetic ritual's sequence and structure, you can begin testing out the different types of rituals. Some of the following exercises are meant to be quick and easy rituals that can be used to supplement the longer, more comprehensive rituals that form the backbone of Kemetic practice. These are only a small selection of what you can do. There are many more rituals dedicated to other forces and invoking any of the 1,500 gods beyond the Neteru. Start fortifying your spiritual connection to the hidden world around you with these exercises:

Morning Devotional to Ra

This is a devotional ritual to Ra that you can do every morning. It works best if you remain consistent and don't miss a day. Since it's a truncated, informal ritual, you don't need to do much prep work, and you can do it in less time than it takes for a pot of coffee to brew. Start by bringing a candle to an empty room. Light the candle and recite the following:

"Hail Ra, Giver of Life! I honor the light and ask for guidance today."

Visualize your body being filled with sunlight for five minutes. Allow it to wash over every part of you, from your fingertips to your toes. Imagine the sunlight converting into energy that gives you clarity and purpose. When you're done, close out the ritual by saying:

"Thank you Ra, Eldest Son of the Eldest. Your guidance shall steer me true. As always, I am in your debt."

Blow out the candle, and then you can go about your daily routine.

Symbol Activation Ritual

This is an activation ritual for a sacred symbol. Choose one of the sacred Kemetic symbols, such as the ankh, djed pillar, was-scepter, tyet knot, scarab, or Eye of Horus. You can draw, paint, carve, or print out a picture of the symbol to serve as its physical representation. Follow the standard ritual sequence, and pick a deity associated with your chosen sacred symbol. The intention you have for the symbol will also influence which god is part of the ritual. Make sure to use an appropriate offering for them.

When you reach step 6 of the ritual, pick up your sacred symbol. Hold it in your hands and picture it glowing with divine energy. Think about your intention for it and recite an activation chant, such as the following:

"Awakened symbol of power, guide and strengthen me."

Repeat the chant 7 times. The number 7 is considered sacred in Ancient Egyptian mythology, representing completeness and perfection. After closing out the ritual, your sacred symbol will be activated. Carry the activated symbol around with you, or put it in a place where its power can further your intention.

Kemetic Protection Amulet

This ritual combines aspects of a protection and activation ritual. It will activate the power of an object bearing a sacred symbol and use that power to protect the caster. Start by carving the Eye of Horus onto the surface of a small object. This is going to be your amulet. Follow the standard ritual sequence, using Ma'at and Sekhmet as the gods whose power will help you unlock the protective magic of the amulet. Offerings of beer, bread, or frankincense will appeal to both of them.

When you get to step 6, pick up your amulet. Hold it in your hands, close your eyes, and visualize a shield of light around it. Recite the following:

"Charge this symbol with the power of Ma'at and Sekhmet. May it guard and protect."

Repeat the prayer three times. In Ancient Egyptian mythology, 3 was linked to the god Horus and represented wisdom and awareness of the divine. Close out the ritual to finish activating your amulet. Activated protection amulets work best when they're kept on or near the caster.

Eye of Horus Protection Spell

This is a protection spell that also uses the power of the Eye of Horus sacred symbol. However, you will call upon Horus himself for this spell. Draw, paint, or print out a picture of the Eye of Horus symbol and set it down in front of you on your altar or sacred space. Place a candle behind the symbol and arrange your offerings. You can use milk, honey, and tea for this spell. Once your preparations are complete, light the candle and open the ritual.

For step 6, start by visualizing a golden light radiating from the Eye of Horus, forming a protective barrier around you. Chant a simple invocation asking for safety and balance. Here's an example:

Udjat Netjer! Udjat Heru!
Eye of the Falcon, bright with flame,
Born of wrath, born of light,
Strike down chaos; shield my name.
Oh Glorious Eye, restored and whole,
Healer of wounds, defender of soul,
Shine upon me with Sekhem might,
Burn away the shadows of night.
Eye of Horus, watcher of skies,
Let no harm beneath you rise.
Seal my flesh, guard my breath,
Turn aside the hand of death.
Wadjet of flame, lash of divine,
Circle me in sacred sign.
As Heru stood, so too shall I,
Strong of voice, with head held high.
I am protected by the Eye that sees,
The Eye that strikes, the Eye that frees.
Nothing evil may approach,
Nothing false may encroach.
Dua Udjat! Dua Heru!
May your light walk before me,
May your fire walk behind me,
May your strength dwell within me.
So it is. So it endures. In maat.

Repeat the chant three times while focusing on your intention of protection. Close the ritual with gratitude and extinguish the flame of the candle. You are now under Horus's protection.

Cleansing and Renewal Ritual with the Ankh

This is a cleansing ritual focusing on the ankh sacred symbol. Get or make a representation of the ankh. It can be a charm, amulet, sigil, statue, or picture bearing the image of an ankh. You will ask Osiris for help with this ritual. Offerings of wine, cedarwood, or myrrh are a good choice. Make sure you face east when performing the ritual since you want to invoke the rebirth and renewal aspect of Osiris.

Hold or place your ankh near a bowl of fresh water and begin the ritual. At step 6, imagine it's glowing with powerful life force energy. Recite the following simple chant:

"Ankh of Life, renew my spirit and cleanse away all that no longer serves me."

Repeat the chant 13 times. The number 13 is a sacred number associated with Osiris and the afterlife. After you're done chanting, dip your fingers into the bowl, then touch them to your forehead, anointing yourself with the purified water. Visualize your mind, body, and soul being cleansed, revitalized, and renewed by the sacred energy of the ankh. Make sure to thank Osiris with the following:

"Thank you, Osiris, Ruler of Eternity. I am made clean and feel renewed by your grace and the divine power of the Ankh of Life."

Close out the ritual. You can either keep the ankh or dispose of it respectfully. If you wish to dispose of it, your options are cremation or burial. For cremation, burn the ankh safely and scatter the ashes in an eastern wind or near a willow tree. For burial, dig a hole near vegetation like a tamarisk, Easter lily, sunflower, iris, daisy, peony, or willow tree.

Healing Spell of Isis

This is a spell that asks Isis to help heal you with the power of heka. Use offerings of a tyet knot, rose, date fig, sweet wine, or saffron. You will also need a bowl of purified water. If you want to use traditional medicine with your spell, include the items you intend to take or apply (bandage, cream, pills, etc.). Arrange them on your altar or sacred space and begin the ritual.

When you reach step 6, pick up the bowl of purified water. While holding it in front of you, visualize Isis' energy flowing from within your core, traveling down your arms to your hands and from your hands into the water. Recite this healing spell for purification and renewal:

Dua Aset! Great Isis, She of Ten Thousand Names,
Healer of the Sick, Mother of Magic,
Whose words brought Osiris to rise again,
Come to me now on wings of breath,
Cloaked in stars and crowned with wisdom.
You who know the secret names,
You who command the power of life,
You who nursed Horus and made him whole,
Place your hands upon me as you did for him.
Draw out pain as you drew poison from his veins,
Banish all illness, all shadow, all fear.
Let your milk become my strength,
Let your tears become my renewal.
Speak my name into the fabric of maat,
That I may be restored, justified, and whole
By your heka, by your breath, by your name,
Heal me, Oh Lady of Life, and let no harm remain.
So I speak. So it is. Under your wings, I rise again.
Dua Aset! Dua Nebet-Hekau! Dua Weret-Hekau!
Praise to Isis! Praise to the Lady of Magic!
Praise to the heka that fills my soul and the eternal balance of maat!

The water is now charged with healing power. Put the bowl down and wash your hands and face with it. If you are healing a physical injury or ailment, wash it with the water as well if medically permissible. Whisper your intention to release your pain and welcome balance. If you have any medical items, anoint them with the water and take the medicine or apply the treatment to your injury or ailment. When you're done, show your gratitude by reciting the following:

"Thank you, Isis, for your nurturing energy and divine spirit. Thank you for the healing power of heka."

Close out the ritual and dispose of any remaining water respectfully. You can pour it into a natural water source or on a clear patch of fertile soil. *Do not* pour it down a drain or into a toilet, as that would be taken as a severe offense by the gods.

Kemetic Spell for Guidance and Clarity

This is a spell invoking the power of Thoth for guidance and clarity. You'll get the best results by performing the ritual at dusk or during the witching hour. Having a full moon on a clear night is ideal but not required. Use offerings of sweet fruit, chocolate, lavender, or writing implements. You should choose a spot in the moonlight to perform the ritual, if possible, as it symbolizes Thoth's wisdom and illumination. Create a sacred space near a window or outside near a persea or evergreen tree.

Place a candle in front of you and light it to start the ritual. Make your intention known by asking the question you wish to answer or the problem you want to solve. Upon arriving at step 6, you will give the following invocation:

"Thoth, Scribe of the Divine, please guide me on my path. May your wisdom be my light, warding off the darkness of ignorance and confusion. Show me the way forward, bringing clarity to my mind and purpose to my steps."

Repeat the invocation 3 times to strengthen your connection to Thoth and gain insight into what it is you seek. While sitting quietly and reflecting, jot down any thoughts you have in a journal. You can use the entry you write to gain insight into your state of mind. Doing this during the ritual will enhance your senses and emotions, allowing you to cut to the heart of the matter. Thoth's energy will flow through your consciousness, bringing the truth to the surface so you can find clarity and guidance. When you're done, close out the ritual and thank Thoth gratefully for his assistance.

Seasonal Kemetic Abundance Ritual

The purpose of this ritual is to encourage abundance in your life during the seasons of birth, renewal, and growth. Perform it in the spring or summer, ideally around the time that crops and flowers are blooming. You will honor either Osiris or Hathor to attract abundance. The best offerings to use are fresh fruits or flowers. If you're performing the ritual in the spring, you should honor Osiris and face eastward. During the summer, honor Hathor and face to the south.

Before you enact the ritual, collect these 4 items: incense (cedarwood, amber or cinnamon), a bowl of purified water, a handful of fertile soil, and a feather. Arrange your offerings and begin the ritual. Hold your intention to seek abundance in your mind. Give praise to Osiris or Hathor and invoke their power by reciting the following:

"Osiris/Hathor, I humbly seek your blessing to bring me abundance. I am grateful for your gifts and promise to share my good fortune with others to spread the glory of your power."

Continue the ritual, and when you reach step 6, chant these words:

"Osiris/Hathor, grant me the same boon you give to the flowers, plants, and trees. May the blessing of the Neteru flow abundantly into my life."

Repeat this chant four times, invoking the Ancient Egyptian sacred number and its association with the seasons, cardinal directions, and elements. Now, you can use the four items you collected earlier. Take the following actions and speak the associated prayer:

- Place the feather to the north. If you're facing east, put it on your left, and if you're facing south, put it behind you and say, *"From the North, I call the winds that carry in the clean air."*
- Place the handful of fertile soil to your right if facing east, and in front of you if facing south, then say, *"From the South, I call the earth where life takes root."*
- Place the bowl of purified water in front of you if you're facing east. If you're facing south, put it on your left and say, *"From the East, I call the waters that clean and nourish."*
- Light the incense and place it to the west. If you're facing east, put it behind you. If you're facing south, put it on your right and say, *"From the West, I call the fires that purify and renew."*

After all your items are placed, take a few minutes to reflect on how the elements help to bring about abundance. When you're done, show your gratitude by reciting the following:

"Thank you, Osiris/Hathor, for your generous blessings. I am grateful for all that you give me."

Blow out the incense and close the ritual. Afterward, you can dispose of the elemental items. Let the incense burn out completely and collect the ashes. If you cremate the feather, do the same and spread the ashes by a willow tree during the spring, a sycamore tree during the summer, or near a patch of plentiful flowers. If you don't burn the feather, bury it in the ground or leave it near a nesting area so the birds or other critters can use it as building material. Return the fertile soil to where you collected it, and pour the water into a pond, lake, river, or stream.

Chapter 6: Mysteries of Life, Death, and Rebirth

One of the most profound aspects of Kemetic spirituality is the philosophical meditation on the cyclical nature of existence. You can find cycles everywhere around you – the seasons, nature, day and night, planetary rotations, and stars going supernova, leading to the birth of a new star. Ancient Egyptians had a unique perspective on the various cycles of life and death. Their myths, rituals, and beliefs all center around the eternal truth that all things live, all things die, and all things are reborn to start the cycle anew. Kemetism incorporates many of these elements into its own belief system. Throughout your spiritual journey, taking the time to explore these principles will help you achieve personal growth and bring your life into balance.

Black Eye Galaxy.[58]

Ancient Egyptians and the Cycle of Life and Death

The key to understanding how Ancient Egyptians viewed the cycle of life and death is to look at what they saw as the purpose of existence. All of a person's deeds were built up throughout their mortal life. They were recorded within the heart and soul, able to be read and judged after they died. Once they received their judgment, if their soul was deemed worthy, they got to move on to the next phase of existence. The cycle of life is repeated in all things, like plants, weather, seasons, days, months, years, planets, stars, and even events or societies.

Look at the rise and fall of civilizations, from Ancient Egypt to Ancient Rome, the empires of Europe, Asia, Africa, and South America. You can see that the Ancient Egyptians were onto something. Likely, our modern civilizations will eventually fall, and new ones will take their place. So it's gone since humans first started banding together in tribes, and it will continue until the last human in the universe closes their eyes in eternal slumber.

The sun will eventually swallow the Earth and the rest of our solar system. It'll go supernova and burn out before collapsing into itself to become a black hole. The universe will reach a point of critical mass and eventually implode, bringing its life cycle to an end. Yet the force of that implosion could echo back out, initiating another "Big Bang" and kick-starting a new universe. If the Ancient Egyptians were right, the cycle will keep repeating for eternity.

Views on Life

To Ancient Egyptians, life was merely one stage in the eternal cycle of existence. Its purpose was to cultivate balance according to the principles of maat in preparation for the journey to the afterlife. Being part of the living world was only temporary, but they didn't fear it coming to an end. However, that didn't mean they sought out death or had no care for the well-being of the living. A longer

Ankh Symbols on a Fragment of Cloth.⁴⁴

life meant more time to perform great deeds and achieve balance, giving them a shot at better rewards when it came time for their soul to be judged.

Scarab Beetle Amulet.⁶⁵

Views on Death

Death was viewed as a transitionary period by Ancient Egyptians. A person's existence didn't end when they perished. Instead, their soul moved on to the afterlife, often guided by one of the gods like Anubis or Hathor, who acted as a psychopomp. Ancient Egyptians believed death was just one stage in the eternal cycle. It was also a necessary experience since they would never get a chance to enjoy their reward for living a balanced life if they didn't die. The living had no way of reaching the underworld; only the souls of departed mortals and gods were able to travel there.

Views on Rebirth and Eternal Life

Ancient Egyptian religious doctrine outlined three major beliefs concerning the afterlife:

1. The existence of the Duat and the underworld.
2. The potential for eternal life.
3. The possibility of a soul being reborn.

The way Ancient Egyptians approached the concept of rebirth is interesting when compared to other religions that believe in rebirth and reincarnation. Because the cycle of life and death drove on endlessly, souls could be reborn in the living world. That gave them another chance to earn their way into A'aru. Their objective was to improve their standing with each new life until they would ultimately be deemed worthy to move on to the Field of Reeds.

A soul transitioning from one stage of their existence to the next was also considered a type of rebirth. After a person died, they would be given a proper burial and funerary rites. This ensured the departed soul would be reborn in the afterlife. When a soul was permitted to enter A'aru, they would be reborn in the Field of Reeds to start their new life in a place without any of the negative aspects of the mortal realm.

Cycle of Life and Death in the Natural World

Ancient Egyptians felt that the cycle of life and death was as apparent in the natural world as it was in human beings. All living things, including plants, flowers, trees, animals, insects, bacteria, and any other type of organism, proceed through the life cycle. The months cycled through each year, as did the seasons. The weather operated on a cycle, with the ebb and flow of heavy rains and droughts.

The Nile River went through a similar cycle, experiencing flooding from the heavy rains during the summer and autumn and receding in the spring. This made the Nile part of an ecological cycle, where the flood waters carried nutrients to the soil along its banks, and when the waters subsided, it left behind fertile land ripe for agriculture. The floods meant death to any crops growing on its banks, but they were reborn thanks to those same floods, which made the land rich with nourishment.

Nile Flood Plains.[56]

If the weather was particularly dry in the summer, it would cause the plants and crops to die. If the plants died, the animals that ate them would die. The humans who depended on the crops and animals to provide them with food would also die. If humans died, society would crumble. Without a society, there would be no culture. No culture meant no religion, and no religion meant no gods. Without the gods, all of existence would cease to be. The only way to prevent such a cataclysm was for the world to remain balanced. A drought might kill some plants, animals, and people, but that made room for the survivors to thrive.

There was an interconnectedness to the cycle of life and death. Everything went through its own life cycle, but it affected the cycle of other parts of the world. It's like a giant spider web - picture the individual cycles as the concentric spirals and the effect they have on each other as the radial and mooring threads. When you look at the web in its entirety, you can see how everything fits neatly into the frame, every thread working in concert to create an efficient system. The universe is like the frame of the spider web, and everything else within it operates based on the same cyclical design.

Ancient Egyptians and the Soul

The Ancient Egyptian conception of the soul evolved over the 3,000 years of the kingdom's existence. From the different funerary texts discovered and deciphered by Egyptologists, the Ancient Egyptian religion believed that the soul was divided into eight parts: the Khet, the Sah, the Ren, the Ka, the Ba, the Ib, the Shuyet, and the Sekhem. They each represented an aspect of a person's totality. Collectively, these eight aspects were called the Akh. All eight parts needed to work together and find balance between them. It was understood that part of a soul's journey in the afterlife was reuniting its eight aspects so they could be made whole again.

Components of the Soul

- **The Khet**: This is a person's physical body. It was believed that the Khet was required for a soul to have consciousness and intelligence in the afterlife. The practice of preserving and mummifying the dead was a direct result of this belief.
- **The Sah**: This is a person's spiritual body. As long as the Khet was properly preserved, the Sah would exist as the vessel through which the person could interact with the afterlife.
- **The Ren**: This is a person's name. Words and names were believed to hold special power. A name was directly related to the person's individuality and standing in the afterlife. Names of the deceased were often etched onto statues or pictures depicting them to aid them in the afterlife. Destroying representations of a person's name was sometimes used as a method to hinder the activities of the departed soul by their enemies.
- **The Ka**: This is a person's life force and core essence. It was thought that the Ka entered a person's Khet just prior to their birth. The Ka leaving the physical body and transitioning to the

afterlife was seen as the necessary action for a person to die. It needed sustenance to survive in the afterlife, which was why the practice of leaving offerings of food and drink came into being.

- **The Ba:** This is a person's personality. It also contained their character traits, intelligence, likes, and dislikes. The Ba was believed to have the ability to freely travel between the physical world and the underworld, using their tomb as a gateway. The most common depiction of the Ba is of a bird with a human head, representing the fact that it was capable of moving from one realm to the other.

- **The Ib:** This is a person's heart. Every deed and action from their life was recorded on the Ib, and it was the part of the soul that was used to render a judgment of their fate. As with their physical body, Ancient Egyptians believed that a person's heart needed to be preserved after death. It would be returned to the mummified corpse, and a heart scarab amulet was placed above it as a means of protection.

- **The Shuyet:** This is a person's shadow. The Ancient Egyptian religion believed that since a person's shadow was present their entire life, it continued on with them into the afterlife. They also thought that a soul could enter the living world during the day with their Shuyet, appearing in the form of a literal shadow. It wasn't considered a very substantive existence, but they had to acknowledge that a shallow existence was still a form of existence.

- **The Sekhem:** This is a person's power. Everyone was said to possess an innate potential for magic, and that potential manifested as the Sekhem. Once a soul has passed all their judgments, the Sekhem would serve as their life force after being reborn in A'aru.

- **The Akh:** This is what a person's soul becomes after being reunited in the afterlife. It's considered a higher form of the soul, having been elevated by passing the trials set forth in the Duat. However, the transformation into the Akh was only possible if all the burial rituals and funerary rites were properly executed. Ancient Egyptians believed that an improper burial or desecration of the tomb would cause the deceased's akh to become a wandering ghost.

Isis and Osiris Myth

The myth of Isis and Osiris was an instructive story meant to explain how the system of the afterlife worked. The tale begins with Osiris, his wife Isis, and his brother Set. Osiris ruled over the kingdom with Isis at his side, and all was good. When they began discussing having a child to give Osiris an heir, he was elated at the prospect. However, in his contentment, he was ignorant of the dark desires hiding deep within his brother's heart. Set burned with jealousy, as he craved power. He wanted to sit on Osiris' throne, and he wanted to claim Isis for himself.

Set went to visit Osiris and got his brother alone. They talked about many things, with Set feigning a moment of vulnerability to deceive Osiris into letting his guard down. As soon as the opportunity presented itself, Set struck his brother down. He murdered Osiris in cold blood and proceeded to dismember the dead god, cutting him into 14 different pieces. Set then scattered the pieces all across Egypt to prevent his brother from returning to life.

With the king dead, Set was able to take the throne. When Isis discovered what Set had done, she fled from the palace. Set ordered his warriors to find her and bring her back to him, but she managed to evade them all, escaping to freedom in the wilds. She recruited Nephthys to help her find the missing pieces of Osiris' body. They enlisted other gods to search every inch of Egypt. Isis and Nephthys traveled from nome to nome, and eventually managed to collect all 14 pieces.

Isis reassembled her husband's body and used her powerful magic to resurrect him from the dead. Upon his return to the land of the living, Osiris was able to finally sire an heir. Isis became pregnant with their son, Horus. Although Osiris was restored to life, he had transformed from what he once was. He was alive, but he was also still part of the afterlife. As a consequence of his dual nature, he was forever bound to the land of the dead. Instead of reclaiming his throne from the murderous Set, Osiris returned to the underworld.

After giving birth, Isis raised her son in secret, telling him about his uncle's crimes. Horus began

Isis Nursing Horus.[87]

training at a young age, honing his combat skills so that when the time came, he could avenge his father's murder. He grew up strong and had a fierce sense of honor and justice. The throne was his right by birth, but Set was still the king. Under Set's tyrannical rule, Egypt descended into chaos and violence.

Once Horus was ready to face his uncle, he journeyed to the palace. Set's warriors attempted to bar him from entry, but he slew every last one of them. There was nothing else standing between him and vengeance. He confronted Set in the throne room and issued his challenge. Set, the god of violence, laughed at his nephew's impertinence. None had ever bested him in a fight, and he had no doubt that Horus, too, would fall at his feet.

The battle between the two gods was savage, with neither combatant giving an inch. Their fight went on for days, and the clash of their weapons reverberated across the kingdom like thunder. The people hid in their homes, fearing a massive storm had come to their lands. In their fury, Horus and Set mutilated each other - Set cut out his nephew's eye, and Horus removed his uncle's manhood. Neither of these injuries did anything to stop the brutal duel.

The other gods heard the sound of the thunder and followed it back to the palace. There, they convened to witness the fight. Isis arrived and used her magic to give her son a boost of strength. This boon was enough for Horus' next strike to tear right through Set's defenses, shattering his weapon into pieces. Seizing the opportunity, Horus drove his blade into Set's forehead. Finally defeated, Set capitulated to his opponent. When Horus pulled his blade out of Set's head, the god Thoth emerged fully formed.

Horus reclaimed his father's throne and took his place as the eternal king. He made Thoth his official scribe, and together, they established the kingdom's first system of laws. Set was judged to have broken the law by usurping Osiris' throne, so he was banished from Egypt and forced to dwell in the barren, foreign lands beyond the kingdom's borders. As Horus brought order to the living world, his father did the same in the afterlife. Osiris took his place as the king of the underworld and judge of the dead. Isis healed her son's mutilated eye, which became the symbolic Eye of Horus.

The Duat and the Afterlife

The Duat is the name given to the underworld by Ancient Egyptians. It was frequently depicted as a subterranean realm covered in darkness. A long tunnel stretched from the entrance to the Hall of Truth, where the Weighing of the Heart ritual took place. However, there were several paths departed souls could take during their journey, and they would have to pass through 12 gates to reach their final destination. It was filled with trials that challenged the soul, forcing them to confront their actions in life and reflect on their connection to maat. It was ultimately Osiris who would judge their fate.

Journey Through the Duat

While there was only one entrance to the Duat, that entrance was accessed through the tombs of the deceased. There were many tombs all across Egypt, but each soul could only pass through their own tomb. Once a soul entered the underworld, they were forced onto a path designated for them based on their status in life. Only pharaohs were afforded passage on a boat. Before setting off on their journey, the souls needed to reunite their eight aspects and transform into the Akh.

The 12 Gates of the Underworld

Each of the 12 gates of the Duat had a sentinel guarding them. These sentinels were gods who were charged with protecting the underworld and determining if a soul was permitted to pass. A trial would be set for the souls at the gates, and they had to successfully complete their trials before the guard allowed them through. Souls that failed their trials were stuck at the gate until they tried again and completed it. After passing the trial at the final gate, the souls were admitted into the Hall of Truth, where Osiris awaited them.

Depiction of a Gate of Duat.[48]

The Weighing of the Heart

Osiris performed the Weighing of the Heart ritual. The god of the dead was assisted in his task by the Assessors of Ma'at, a collection of 42 minor deities that resided in the hall. The soul first needed to prove their devotion by addressing every single god by name. If the soul proved themselves true, Osiris and the Assessors proceeded to read the deeds recorded on the soul's heart. The judges then decided whether or not the soul was ready for the weighing. Those deemed ready submitted themselves to the authority of Osiris.

He placed the soul's Ib on one side of his scale and the Feather of Ma'at on the other side. If the Ib was heavier than the Feather, the soul was deemed to be unbalanced, and they were fed to the demon goddess Ammit, who gnawed away at the souls until nothing of them remained. If the scales were balanced, Osiris sent the soul to be reborn in the living realm, where they would get a chance to raise their status and add more deeds to their heart. If the Ib was lighter than the Feather, the soul was allowed to pass into A'aru.

A'aru

A'aru is the Field of Reeds, the paradise realm that serves as the reward for souls that are judged to be in balance with maat. The souls are reborn in A'aru with a new perfect body. There is no pain, no sadness, no anger or jealousy or greed. Souls would get to spend their time doing their ideal job and indulging in any hobby they desire. They're also reunited with their loved ones who passed the Weighing of the Heart. These souls get to spend the rest of eternity living in total bliss.

Ancient Egyptian Festivals

There were many festivals celebrated by Ancient Egyptians throughout the year. They enjoyed communal gatherings and having an excuse to feast. At the end of each festival, a notch was made on the staff of Thoth. This was how they tracked the progression of the year. When the time came to repeat the first festival, they knew that a year had passed. Coming back around to celebrate the festivals again tied into their belief in the cyclical nature of the universe. Here's a list of the main Ancient Egyptian festivals:

1. **Wepet-Renpet Festival (The Opening of the Year):** This was the first festival of the year, not unlike the modern New Year's Day. Feasts would be held by the Nile River, but flooding could change their exact location from year to year. As a new year was being reborn, Osiris was honored at the festival, focusing on his rebirth.

2. **Wag Festival (Osiris Death Festival):** This festival was held after the Wepet-Renpet Festival. It was dedicated to the death of Osiris. Ancient Egyptians constructed little paper boats and placed them on graves, making sure they faced westward. Paper shrines were also floated down the Nile as a way to honor Osiris' death.
3. **Thoth Festival:** This festival celebrated the birth of Thoth following Horus' victory over his uncle Set. Ancient Egyptians honored Thoth by making offerings to him and giving his symbols a place of prominence during the feasts.
4. **Tekh Festival (The Feast of Drunkenness):** This festival honored the goddess Hathor in her aspect of the Lady of Drunkenness. The Tekh Festival was similar to modern Germany's Oktoberfest, as beer drinking was the central feature of the celebration. Ancient Egyptians used it as an opportunity to cut loose and have fun.
5. **Opet Festival:** This was a very important festival of the Ancient Egyptians. It was when the pharaoh traveled to the city of Thebes – where Amun rejuvenated them. The people feasted and got a chance to ask Amun's statue questions. Priests interpreted the answers given by the god, either relaying the responses from Amun or tipping the statue one way to indicate a positive answer and the other way for a negative one.
6. **Hathor Festival:** This was a festival dedicated to the birth of the goddess Hathor. It was held every year at Dendera, where Hathor's cult was centered. Overindulgence was encouraged, and the Hathor Festival was frequently the cause of a baby boom nine months later. Ancient Egyptians gave thanks to Hathor for her many blessings, especially the blessing of alcohol.
7. **Sokar Festival (Planting Festival):** This festival was dedicated to the god of agriculture, who shared the celebration's name. The Sokar Festival commemorated the planting of crops and the first of nature's blooms. It was later supplanted by the Festival of Khoiak, which was a solemn event where raucous partying was discouraged.
8. **Bast Festival:** This festival celebrated Bastet, the cat goddess who protected women and children. It was very popular with the people of Ancient Egypt, and the feasts were often incredibly elaborate affairs. There was plenty of music, dancing, and other forms of merriment.

9. **Nehebkau Festival**: This was a festival honoring the god Nehebkau, who was responsible for binding the Ka to the Khet just before a baby was born. He also tied the Ka to the Ba upon a person's death. Without him, the cycle of life, death, and rebirth wouldn't be possible.
10. **Min Festival**: This festival celebrated Min, a god of fertility, virility, and conception. Although the human reproductive aspect of the Min Festival was a major part of the processions, Ancient Egyptians also used the feast to ask the god for blessings of prosperity and abundance in their harvests.
11. **Wadi Festival (The Beautiful Feast of the Valley)**: This was the Ancient Egyptian "day of the dead." The people celebrated the festival by visiting the tombs of their loved ones who died. Offerings of food, drink, and flowers were brought to nourish their souls and fortify them for their journey through the afterlife. Statues of the gods Amun, Mut, and Khonsu were taken out of their temples and carried to the necropolises.

Mortuary Temple of Hatshepsut.[59]

12. **Sed Festival**: This was another festival meant to honor the pharaoh and revitalize him. It was only celebrated after a pharaoh had reigned for 30 years. However, following the first celebration, it was held every three years thereafter until the pharaoh died. As part of the festival, the pharaoh had to complete a physical trial to prove they were still fit to rule.

13. **The Epagomenae:** Due to the fact that the Ancient Egyptian year only had 360 days, there were 5 days added to the end of the year to bring it in line with the solar year. Every four years would be a leap year, and they'd add 6 days. These 5 or 6 days were known as "epagomenal days," and they weren't considered part of the actual year. They took on a reputation as being a time of transition when magic was particularly potent. At the end of the Epagomenae, the Wepet-Renpet Festival was held, marking the start of a new year.

Practical Exercises

The question about what happens to us after we die is something that just about everyone asks at one point or another. The philosophy of Ancient Egyptians concerning the cycle of life, death, and rebirth can be comforting. We don't cease to exist at the moment of our demise; we transition into a new state of being. Do the following exercises to help you better grasp the concepts of Ancient Egypt's relationship with the afterlife:

Meditation on the Cycle of Ra

This exercise will ask you to take some time to meditate on the cycle of the sun. Close your eyes and visualize the journey of Ra across the sky and through the underworld. Imagine that you're a part of this eternal cycle, rising from the underworld at dawn, soaring through the heavens throughout the day, and then diving back into the underworld. Now, picture yourself navigating your way through the Duat, sailing along the portion of the Nile River that flows along the tunnels of the underworld. As a mortal practicing Kemetism, you're deeply connected to the cycle of life and death. Focus on the areas of your lives where renewal or clarity is needed. Keep notes in your journal about the experience, allowing you to reflect on the lessons afterward.

The Weighting of the Heart Exercise

This exercise is meant to replicate the Weighing of the Heart ritual. You can serve as your own judge and reflect on the kinds of actions, behaviors, and beliefs that might be recorded in your heart. Think about your acts of kindness, heroic moments, and greatest achievements. Write them down on a piece of paper. Then, list all your regrets, fears, and burdens. Reflect on the two sides of the list and try to determine how your heart would fare against the Feather of Ma'at. This is a good way to assess whether or not your soul is balanced. You can symbolically lighten the weight of your heart by either burning or burying the paper. Visualize those negative thoughts and emotions being purged from your soul and removed from the record in your heart.

Osirian Renewal Ritual

This ritual is dedicated to Osiris. You will ask him for his blessing of renewal. Start by creating a simple altar with green plants and water. Think about what you wish to "resurrect" in your life. Maybe it's hope, creativity, or love. Perhaps you want to pick up an old hobby again, repair a strained relationship, or refresh your professional credentials. Hold your intention in your mind as you open the ritual. When you get to step 6, recite the following chant:

"Osiris, Lord of Renewal, I ask that you guide me through my transformation and rebirth."

Repeat this chant 4 times. Finish up and close out the ritual, thanking Osiris for his blessing. Just remember that change doesn't happen on its own. Osiris can help to renew your interests or desires, but you still need to go out there and make things happen.

Chapter 7: Advanced Kemetic Magic Practices

Understanding the beliefs, rituals, and myths of Kemetism is a good foundation for your spiritual journey. With that in mind, you can start exploring more complex and nuanced aspects of the religion and its magical practices. Although Kemetism draws heavily on the Ancient Egyptian religion and mythology, it's also influenced by other forms of spiritual beliefs and practices. These are more advanced than the rituals, spells, and invocations you've already learned. It can be very difficult to get a handle on some of these techniques, so patience is a must. The reward for your hard work and diligence will be gaining access to a whole new level of magical abilities.

Dreamwork

Kemetic dreamwork is rooted in the Ancient Egyptian practice of oneiromancy, which is the practice of using dreams for divination and guidance. People who experienced detailed dreams with significant imagery and messages were believed to be blessed by the gods. They were held in high regard by society, similar to the Ancient Greek oracles. There were sanctuaries with "dream beds" that could induce prophetic dreams. After receiving one such dream, Thutmose IV, the younger son of the reigning pharaoh, restored the Great Sphinx of Giza and was later chosen to succeed his father over his older brother.

How It Works

The main goal of dreamwork is to decipher the images and emotions of your dreams in order to gain insight into your life, relationships, ambitions, fears, and spiritual beliefs. Your dreams can also grant you knowledge of the world around you and possibly even predict the future. Your subconscious and unconscious minds pick up a lot more information than your conscious mind can process. When you dream, many of those details that you missed while awake will be presented to you in the form of abstract, obscure, and esoteric experiences. Your job as a dreamworker is to sift through the contents of a dream and separate the meaningful from the meaningless.

Sweet Dreams.[60]

Becoming a Dreamworker

You can get started with dreamwork by keeping a dream journal. Make a habit of writing down as much as you can remember about your dreams as soon as you wake up. Dreams will still feel very present in the first moments after you awaken, but they quickly become distant and foggy. Logging as many details as possible will allow you to go back and analyze what you wrote. The fleeting nature of dreams means the majority of people miss out on the messages, warnings, premonitions, and intuitive deductions given to them. The more you practice your dreamwork, the better you'll get at uncovering the mysteries of the deepest parts of your mind.

Dreams from the Neteru

There's no way to guarantee that your dreams will give you premonitions or spiritual insight. However, you can increase your chances of connecting with the Neteru by performing a Kemetic Sleep Ritual. It works best if you call on Isis or Nephthys, as their associations with dreams and the mystical arts will synchronize with your intention. Your offerings should be warm milk, herbal tea, bananas, avocados, cheese, lavender, or frankincense. These foods, drinks, and incense are known for inducing a calm state of mind that will help with the clarity of your dreams.

Follow the standard Kemetic ritual sequence and perform it right before you go to sleep. Make your intention for dreamwork clear by saying:

"I am a dreamworker seeking hidden truths and future paths. Isis/Nephthys, please bless my dreams with the power of heka and give me the wisdom to follow your guidance."

When you reach step 6 of the ritual, recite the following chant:

"Oh great Isis/Nephthys, I am a seeker of knowledge. My mind is open. My dreams are a conduit to the divine."

Repeat the chant seven times, and then take a few minutes to quietly reflect on what you hope to learn through your dreamwork. Make sure you consume any food or drink offerings before you close out the ritual. Place your dream journal and a pen or pencil beside your bed so you'll have easy access to it the moment you awaken. Write down every detail you can remember from your dream, no matter how insignificant or random it might seem. Those little details are often where the messages from the Neteru are hidden.

Shamanic Journeying

A shamanic journey is a trip into the spiritual plane, where you can connect with the forces of nature, the elements, and the cosmos. Nothing about it is straightforward, and even finding an ingress can be extremely difficult. Many have tried and failed, simply giving up on the endeavor altogether. Those who manage to succeed in embarking on a shamanistic journey rarely ever return the same as they left. The very act of entering the spiritual plane requires a transformation, and the secrets and truths revealed there awakens a heightened state of awareness. You never know what you'll discover while on a shamanistic journey, but you can be sure that whatever you find will change your life.

How to Do It

To take a shamanic journey, you first need to enter an altered state of consciousness. This can be achieved in several different ways:

- **Meditation:** Enter a deep meditative state by clearing your mind and focusing on nothing but your breaths. Continue meditating until your mind is completely blank. This will allow you to slip into an altered state of consciousness.

- **Visual Trance Induction (VTI):** Watch VTI videos consisting of hypnotic patterns and colors that continuously change. This triggers different parts of your brain and can induce a trance-like state.

- **Holotropic Breathwork:** Use a controlled breathing technique that shifts the balance of oxygen and carbon dioxide in your body, causing an effect similar to hyperventilation. It consists of quick, rhythmic breaths for an extended period.

- **Binaural Beats:** Listen to audio tracks with headphones or earbuds that play tones of different frequencies in each ear. This creates the illusion of a third tone at a lower frequency, known as a *binaural beat*. It will alter your brainwaves to cause a hypnotic state.

- **Psychedelics:** Take drugs like mushrooms, LSD, or MDMA to completely shift your perceptions and make you susceptible to entering an altered state of mind. This method can have wildly different results for each person, and psychedelics are illegal in most countries. If you decide to try this method anyway, make sure you have someone you trust with you who will remain sober and watch over you.

Start setting up your shamanic journey ritual by choosing a sacred space where you won't have any distractions. Be sure to purify your sacred space to prevent any negative energy or ill-intentioned spirits from interfering with your journey. Place a candle on the ground in front of you and light it. Spend several minutes mentally repeating your intention to go on a shamanic journey. When you're ready to begin the ritual, speak the following invocation:

"I call the Neteru to guide me as I walk the paths through the unknown. Protect me on my journey and deliver me to my destination with an open heart and mind."

Now you can induce an altered state of mind. Use whichever method you prefer. For safety reasons, you should blow out the candle before you begin your shamanic journey. There's no telling what you'll discover, so keep a journal nearby to record your experiences.

Healing Crystals

Healing crystals can be charged with different types of energy and used to provide a number of health benefits. They can help heal an injury, treat anxiety and lower stress, remove negative emotions, and protect you from harm. The way healing crystals work is similar to how Ancient Egyptians used amulets. You need to perform an activation ritual on the crystals to charge them with positive energy and then keep them nearby to receive the benefits. Here's a list of healing crystals, what they can do, and which gods they're associated with:

Healing Crystal	Uses	God/Goddess	Appearance
Agate	Grants harmony, stability, and balance.	Bes	Agate.[61]

Healing Crystal	Uses	God/Goddess	Appearance
Amethyst	Treats stress, anxiety, and insomnia.	Hathor	Amethyst.[63]
Aventurine	Offers balance, mental clarity, and prosperity.	Thoth	Aventurine.[68]
Calcite	Gives energy, vitality, and emotional healing.	Bastet	Calcite.[64]
Carnelian	Promotes creativity, courage, and motivation.	Horus	Carnelian Quartz.[65]

Healing Crystal	Uses	God/Goddess	Appearance
Citrine	Boosts happiness, vitality, and optimism.	Ra	Citrine.[66]
Fluorite	Helps with focus and organization; prevents diseases.	Sekhmet	Fluorite Quartz.[67]
Hematite	Wards off negative energy and spirits.	Shu	Hematite Quartz.[68]
Labradorite	Enhances spiritual energy, magical abilities, and intuition.	Isis	Labradorite.[69]

Healing Crystal	Uses	God/Goddess	Appearance
Lapis Lazuli	Increases intuition, communication, and spiritual awareness.	Ma'at	Lapis Lazuli.[70]
Moonstone	Bolsters intuition, feminine energy, and prophetic dreams.	Nephthys	Moonstone.[71]
Selenite	Clears or enhances the energy from other crystals.	Osiris	Selenite Cluster.[72]
Tourmaline	Protects against negative energy.	Geb	Schorl Tourmaline.[73]

Sound Healing

Sound healing uses specific frequencies, tones, and vibrations to help you relax, reduce your stress, and improve your overall well-being. This is usually achieved using instruments like singing bowls, bells and chimes, tuning forks, or gongs, although it's also possible to use vocal toning. Sound healing isn't music in the traditional sense since the emphasis is on resonance and vibrations instead of melodies and rhythm. The sound frequencies from the instruments synchronize with your brainwaves, interrupting negative thought patterns and resetting them to a neutral state.

Sound baths are a common form of sound healing, where you lay flat on your back while others surrounding you bathe you in the sounds of their instruments. Singing bowls, bells, chimes, and tuning forks are struck to create tones and vibrations. Vocal toning employs mostly elongated vowels and simple tones to create vibrations in the back of your throat. Humming can have a similar effect on your body and mind. The goal is to focus on the sensations of the resonating sounds, allowing them to soothe you. Deep breathing can help with further relaxation, and sound healing is often paired with meditation.

Singing Bowl from Nepal.[74]

Nezu Museum Gong.[75]

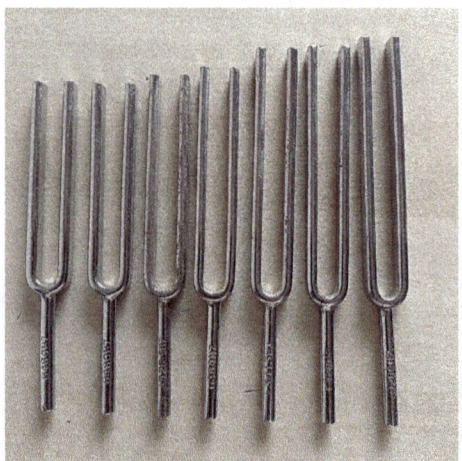

Tuning Forks.[76]

Sacred Geometry

Ancient Egyptians had a relatively comprehensive understanding of mathematics and geometry. While most of their math was focused on practical uses, like record keeping, tax collection, architecture, construction, and agriculture, they had a sense that numbers could be imbued with spiritual meaning. In addition to sacred numbers, they also believed in the existence of sacred geometry. When constructing the pyramids, temples, tombs, and other structures, they were always careful to adhere to certain geometric principles that carried divine connotations.

Panorama of the Sphinx and Pyramids of Giza.[77]

The Great Pyramid of Giza was built using the Golden Ratio, the Fibonacci sequence, and Pythagorean Theorem. The Temple of Amun was designed to mimic the human body, which is famous for its naturally occurring Golden Ratio proportions. Although these sacred geometric theories were codified later by the Greeks and Italians, it's clear the Ancient Egyptians recognized the same principles. Plato described the Golden Ratio in all but name when he called it a fundamental principle of the universe, and he had spent 13 years studying geometry in Egypt, while Pythagoras was there for 22 years. It's entirely possible their work was inspired by the Ancient Egyptians.

Kemetism builds on the knowledge of the Ancient Egyptians and combines it with later advancements in mathematical theories to present a refined version of sacred geometry. The sacred geometric pattern known as the Flower of Life is made up of 19 equal circles - 1 circle in the middle and 18

The Flower of Life.[78]

surrounding it – that overlap in order to create a floral pattern. It's the perfect expression of the Kemetic belief in cycles, as the circles of the Flower of Life repeat, connect, and work together to create a beautiful design.

Mandalas are another aspect of sacred geometry that Kemetism uses to aid in spiritual exploration. They are created using various geometric shapes that start around a central point and are gradually built out, resulting in intricate and unique designs. The interconnectedness of mandalas represents the workings of the universe and how many different patterns come together to produce a complex, synchronistic system. They are often used for meditation and spiritual rituals, helping to calm the mind and keep it focused. You can apply these concepts to your own practices, especially when reflecting on the workings of the universe.

Sun Mandala.[79]

Building a Personal Connection to the Neteru

If you want to forge a personal connection to the Neteru, you have to be willing to make sacrifices. You can start by employing long-term devotional practices. Every day, no matter where you are or what you're doing, you must drop everything in order to perform devotional rituals for the Neteru. These can't be the quick and easy kind, either. You need to incorporate prayers, chants, offerings, meditation, and spiritual reflection. It's also necessary to construct a permanent altar in a dedicated sacred space. Your altar should include symbols and icons of the Neteru. Another way to show your devotion to them is through creative endeavors. Art, poetry, music, dance, and storytelling are all great ways to express your dedication to serving the Neteru.

Joining the priesthood is an option for those willing to devote even more of themselves to the gods. Most branches of Kemetism have a dedicated priesthood that's responsible for leading rituals, teaching initiates, and maintaining sacred spaces in temples or other areas of worship. There are often strict requirements to join the priesthood. You need to undergo training, prove your knowledge of Kemetic theological doctrine, fully grasp the central tenets of the religion, and be well-versed in the procession of all types of rituals. Once you are initiated into the priesthood, you'll have to work your way up each level before you can serve as a high priest.

Designing Your Own Rituals

Designing your own Kemetic rituals requires a comprehensive understanding of many different aspects of the religion. Knowing how each part of the ritual sequence connects and builds on the previous step is essential. You should also be able to recognize and identify many of the symbols, icons, concepts, and deities. A good place to start is with the standard Kemetic ritual. Dissect its structure, taking note of the interplay between recitations, offerings, and symbols of power. Here are some ideas you can use when creating your own advanced rituals:

Multiple Neteru Symbols

People typically stick to a single symbol of the Neteru in their rituals. It keeps things simple and doesn't risk causing confusion or offense to the gods. If you want to enhance your connection to them, you can attempt to use multiple Neteru symbols in your rituals. The key thing to remember is that the symbols you choose must be compatible. The attributes of the symbols should be balanced, adhering to the principles of maat.

Lunar Phases

Ancient Egyptians put a lot of effort into following the phases of the moon. They had three different festivals they celebrated each month based on the lunar phases. The phases had their own names and meanings, including:

- **Achet or Ipip (New Moon):** To be dark or invisible
- **Sopdu (Waxing Crescent):** To approach
- **Renenutet (First Quarter):** To harvest or reap
- **Hapi (Waxing Gibbous):** To be content or satisfied
- **Bentyet or Hathor (Full Moon):** To be rounded or full
- **Sekhmet (Waning Gibbous):** To be strong

- **Nehebkau (Third Quarter)**: To weave or braid
- **Sia (Waning Crescent)**: To vanish or disappear

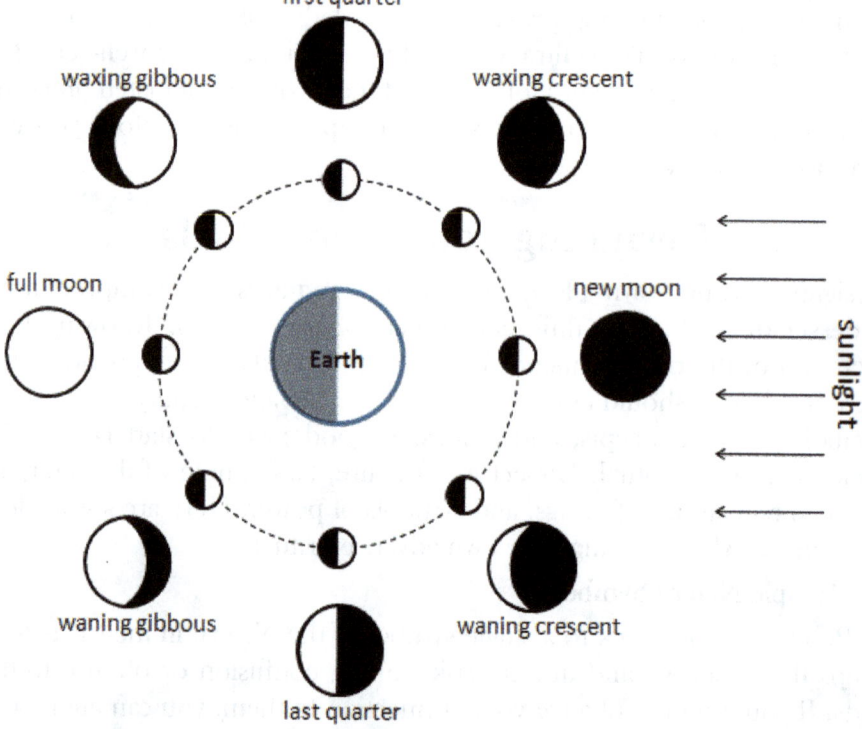

The Lunar Phases.[10]

You can use items that symbolize the phases of the moon in your rituals or perform them during a phase that corresponds to the purpose and deity of the ritual.

Planetary Hours

The ancient astrological system of planetary hours divides the days of the week and hours of the day, assigning rulership over them to the seven classical planets. Kemetism associates those planets with the Neteru as the Ancient Egyptians did. The seven planets and their associated gods are:

- **Saturn:** Geb
- **Jupiter:** Amun
- **Mars:** Horus
- **Venus:** Hathor
- **Mercury:** Thoth

- **The Moon:** Khonsu
- **The Sun:** Ra

Here's the breakdown of the days of the week and the hours of the day in the planetary hours system:

Hour	Sunday	Monday	Tuesday	Wednesday	Thursday	Friday	Saturday
SUNRISE							
1	Ra	Khonsu	Horus	Thoth	Amun	Hathor	Geb
2	Hathor	Geb	Ra	Khonsu	Horus	Thoth	Amun
3	Thoth	Amun	Hathor	Geb	Ra	Khonsu	Horus
4	Khonsu	Horus	Thoth	Amun	Hathor	Geb	Ra
5	Geb	Ra	Khonsu	Horus	Thoth	Amun	Hathor
6	Amun	Hathor	Geb	Ra	Khonsu	Horus	Thoth
7	Horus	Thoth	Amun	Hathor	Geb	Ra	Khonsu
8	Ra	Khonsu	Horus	Thoth	Amun	Hathor	Geb
9	Hathor	Geb	Ra	Khonsu	Horus	Thoth	Amun
10	Thoth	Amun	Hathor	Geb	Ra	Khonsu	Horus
11	Khonsu	Horus	Thoth	Amun	Hathor	Geb	Ra
12	Geb	Ra	Khonsu	Horus	Thoth	Amun	Hathor
SUNSET	Thursday	Friday	Saturday	Sunday	Monday	Tuesday	Wednesday
13	Amun	Hathor	Geb	Ra	Khonsu	Horus	Thoth
14	Horus	Thoth	Amun	Hathor	Geb	Ra	Khonsu
15	Ra	Khonsu	Horus	Thoth	Amun	Hathor	Geb

16	Hathor	Geb	Ra	Khonsu	Horus	Thoth	Amun
17	Thoth	Amun	Hathor	Geb	Ra	Khonsu	Horus
18	Khonsu	Horus	Thoth	Amun	Hathor	Geb	Ra
19	Geb	Ra	Khonsu	Horus	Thoth	Amun	Hathor
20	Amun	Hathor	Geb	Ra	Khonsu	Horus	Thoth
21	Horus	Thoth	Amun	Hathor	Geb	Ra	Khonsu
22	Ra	Khonsu	Horus	Thoth	Amun	Hathor	Geb
23	Hathor	Geb	Ra	Khonsu	Horus	Thoth	Amun
24	Thoth	Amun	Hathor	Geb	Ra	Khonsu	Horus

Seasonal Cycles

Kemetism recognizes both the modern seasonal cycle and the Kemetic solar calendar of Ancient Egypt, which had three seasons:

- **Akhet (Inundation)**: This season was when the Nile River would flood and replenish the nutrients in the fertile soil. Lasts from July to October.

- **Peret (Emergence and Growth)**: This season is when the floods stop, and crops can be planted and cultivated. Lasts from November to February.

- **Shemu (Harvest and Recession)**: This season is when the Nile River recedes, leading to hot, dry weather and possible droughts. Lasts from March to June.

You can use symbols of the Kemetic seasons to tap into their power for your rituals. Reciting prayers, chants, invocations, or devotionals to the Neteru that correspond with each season will strengthen your connection to them. Performing the rituals during those seasons can also make your magic more potent.

Practical Exercises

Wrapping your head around the concepts for advanced Kemetic rituals isn't easy, so it's a good idea to practice them as much as possible. Here are some great exercises to get you started:

Multi-Deity Ritual for Cosmic Balance

For this ritual, you can select a range of deities to include for a variety of purposes. As an example, you could use Ra for vitality, Ma'at for balance, and Hathor for love. You should draw or create symbols that represent each deity and light candles and incense for each Neteru, offering a prayer of intent. Afterward, meditate by envisioning your energies merging into a unified force around you.

Shamanic Journey to the Duat

The Shamanic Journey to the Duat exercise will transition you into a heightened state of spiritual awareness. Place an image of Ra or Anubis to serve as your main guide. Light candles and burn incense that promotes calmness, such as myrrh or frankincense, to help you enter a meditative state. Try to visualize yourself on a boat with Ra, sailing on his lunar barque through the Duat. Imagine traveling through the 12 gates and overcoming the challenges set forth by the guards. See yourself encountering the gods, asking their advice and seeking insights from them. Picture coming across mighty Osiris, God of the Dead and the final judge at the Weighing of the Heart. When Ra finally returns you to the surface, make sure to thank him for guiding you safely through the underworld. Ground yourself by touching the earth in the dream state or holding a stone in your hand. Once you're back in the real world, write down everything you experienced in your journal.

Sacred Geometry Ritual

This ritual will test your knowledge of sacred geometry. You must create a Kemetic geometric symbol or pattern, like a pyramid or djed pillar, using crystals, stones, or drawn diagrams. Sit in front of the symbol or pattern and start meditating. Visualize energy in the form of a golden light flowing through the symbol or pattern and coming into balance with your own energy. You can use your finger or a wand to trace the shape, drawing its energy toward you while chanting affirmations tied to the symbol or pattern's purpose. It can be something like: *"Grant me power and stability as the unwavering pyramid,"* or *"Bring me strength and resilience as the djed stands unshaken."*

Priest/Priestess Dedication Ritual

In this exercise, you're going to create your own ritual in the style of a Kemetic priest or priestess and "offer yourself" to the Neteru of your choosing. You can write your own oath to the gods and speak it out loud after invoking your chosen deity during the ritual. Your oath can be something like: *"I swear by the eternal sun and the boundless sky to devote myself in service to Ra."* You must conclude the ritual with a moment of gratitude, reaffirming your commitment to walk the path of the priesthood with devotion and balance.

Chapter 8: Living in Alignment with Ma'at

Living a life in alignment with the principles of Ma'at means upholding truth, justice, and honor, preserving law and order, and maintaining balance in all things. It also means applying those principles to everything you do. It's not enough to just follow her example when practicing Kemetism. You should evaluate your actions and behavior to see if you have any shortcomings. Everyone has the occasional lapse in judgment, but if you're regularly doing things that are anathema to Ma'at, you need to take a hard look at why you habitually commit unacceptable acts. Even if you believe you are a good person, you likely have areas of your life that are lacking in balance and alignment with Ma'at.

Allegory of Justice.[81]

The Role of Ma'at in Kemetism

Ma'at governs the balance of natural cycles, human relationships, and spiritual truths. She embodies the concepts and ideals of honor and fairness. Her values are the lens through which we examine our own lives and determine how well we measure up. You should strive to harmonize your thoughts, actions, and intentions with the universal laws laid out by Ma'at. That's the only way to achieve equilibrium both within yourself and with the world around you. This is one of the primary guiding forces of Kemetism.

Every Kemetic ritual must adhere to the principles of Ma'at to be successful. Performing rituals or spells with bad intentions throws them off balance. Anyone who participates in actions that bring undue harm to others is going directly against Ma'at. Telling or spreading lies defiles everything she represents. There exists a clear and present danger for those who willingly flout the rules and believe themselves to be above reproach. It can attract evil spirits and negative energy into your heart, mind, and soul. Once they find a way to worm their way into your life, it can be incredibly difficult to get rid of them. The best thing to do is make sure you don't break the laws conveyed to humanity by Ma'at.

42 Laws of Ma'at

The 42 Laws of Ma'at are also known as the 42 Declarations of Innocence or the 42 Negative Confessions. They are laid out in the Ancient Egyptian Book of the Dead and outline the principles of Ma'at, including truth, justice, and order. Departed souls would recite these declarations in the Hall of Truth as part of the ritual of the Weighing of

Kha and Merit Before Osiris (Book of the Dead).[18]

the Heart. A soul needed to prove that they had followed the path of honor and purity before they could submit their heart for judgment.

42 Assessors of Ma'at reside in the Hall of Truth. They are minor gods whose sole purpose is to assist Osiris in his judgments. Each of the Assessors corresponds to one of the 42 Laws of Ma'at. Souls would address them by name and profess that they hadn't broken any of the laws. The Assessors are ostensibly responsible for punishing souls who break the law associated with them, so souls must declare their innocence to each god in turn. Here's the list of the 42 Laws of Ma'at in the form of the declaration of innocence given for them:

1. Hail, Usekh-nemmt, who comest forth from Anu. *I have not committed sin.*
2. Hail, Hept-khet, who comest forth from Kher-aha. *I have not committed robbery with violence.*
3. Hail, Fenti, who comest forth from Khemenu. *I have not stolen.*
4. Hail, Am-khaibit, who comest forth from Qernet. *I have not slain men and women.*
5. Hail, Neha-her, who comest forth from Rasta. *I have not stolen grain.*
6. Hail, Ruruti, who comest forth from Heaven. *I have not purloined offerings.*
7. Hail, Arfi-em-khet, who comest forth from Suat. *I have not stolen the property of the gods.*
8. Hail, Neba, who comest and goest. *I have not uttered lies.*
9. Hail, Set-qesu, who comest forth from Hensu. *I have not carried away food.*
10. Hail, Utu-nesert, who comest forth from Het-ka-Ptah. *I have not uttered curses.*
11. Hail, Qerrti, who comest forth from Amentet. *I have not committed adultery.*
12. Hail, Hraf-haf, who comest forth from thy cavern. *I have made none to weep.*
13. Hail, Basti, who comest forth from Bast. *I have not eaten the heart.*
14. Hail, Ta-retiu, who comest forth from the night. *I have not attacked any man.*
15. Hail, Unem-snef, who comest forth from the execution chamber. *I am not a man of deceit.*

16. Hail, Unem-besek, who comest forth from Mabit. *I have not stolen cultivated land.*
17. Hail, Neb-Maat, who comest forth from Maati. *I have not been an eavesdropper.*
18. Hail, Tenemiu, who comest forth from Bast. *I have not slandered anyone.*
19. Hail, Sertiu, who comest forth from Anu. *I have not been angry without just cause.*
20. Hail, Tutu, who comest forth from Ati. *I have not debauched mine own wife.*
21. Hail, Uamenti, who comest forth from the Khebt chamber. *I have not debauched the wives of other men.*
22. Hail, Maa-antuf, who comest forth from Per-Menu. *I have not polluted myself.*
23. Hail, Her-uru, who comest forth from Nehatu. *I have terrorized none.*
24. Hail, Khemiu, who comest forth from Kaui. *I have not transgressed the law.*
25. Hail, Shet-kheru, who comest forth from Urit. *I have not been angry.*
26. Hail, Nekhenu, who comest forth from Heqat. *I have not shut my ears to the words of truth.*
27. Hail, Kenemti, who comest forth from Kenmet. *I have not blasphemed.*
28. Hail, An-hetep-f, who comest forth from Sau. *I am not a man of violence.*
29. Hail, Sera-kheru, who comest forth from Unaset. *I have not been a stirrer up of strife.*
30. Hail, Neb-heru, who comest forth from Netchfet. *I have not acted with undue haste.*
31. Hail, Sekhriu, who comest forth from Uten. *I have not pried into the matters of others.*
32. Hail, Neb-abui, who comest forth from Sauti. *I have not multiplied my words in speaking.*
33. Hail, Nefer-Tem, who comest forth from Het-ka-Ptah. *I have wronged none; I have done no evil.*

34. Hail, Tem-Sepu, who comest forth from Tetu. *I have not worked witchcraft against the pharaoh.*
35. Hail, Ari-em-ab-f, who comest forth from Tebu. *I have never stopped the flow of a neighbor's water.*
36. Hail, Ahi, who comest forth from Nu. *I have never raised my voice.*
37. Hail, Uatch-rekhit, who comest forth from Sau. *I have not cursed the gods.*
38. Hail, Neheb-ka, who comest forth from thy cavern. *I have not acted with arrogance.*
39. Hail, Neheb-nefert, who comest forth from thy cavern. *I have not stolen the bread of the gods.*
40. Hail, Tcheser-tep, who comest forth from the shrine. *I have not carried away the khenfu cakes from the spirits of the dead.*
41. Hail, An-af, who comest forth from Maati. *I have not snatched away the bread of the child nor treated with contempt the god of my city.*
42. Hail, Hetch-abhu, who comest forth from Ta-she. *I have not slain the cattle belonging to the gods.*

Applications of the Principles of Ma'at

Following the principles of Ma'at isn't the only thing you can do when practicing Kemetism to gain access to A'aru in the afterlife. There are practical applications in your daily life that can serve to both enhance your spiritual status and make your interactions, relationships, and experiences run more smoothly. Being honest and fair with your family, friends, neighbors, acquaintances, and coworkers will allow you to cultivate a reputation of trustworthiness, respectability, and reliability. People will know that you're someone they can depend on when they need someone they know will tell the truth, act without bias, treat them well, and follow through on your promises.

Merits of Following Ma'at

Having a positive reputation has plenty of advantages. Others will be more likely to give you the benefit of the doubt in situations where they might question another person's motives or intentions. You'll be taken at your word more often rather than constantly being forced to show proof of what you say. Your coworkers will be more pleasant and willing to collaborate with you, and you'll have a better chance of being given more power and responsibilities by your superiors. When you treat people well, they're more likely to treat you well in return.

That's not to say that you won't encounter any problems when following the principles of Ma'at. Problems are bound to arise in your relationships. However, staying true to the ideals of justice, honesty, and balance is the best way to resolve those conflicts. When you make a mistake or hurt someone's feelings, you should take accountability and apologize immediately. Don't allow negative emotions to fester. Anger, frustration, bitterness, and jealousy can close off your heart and darken your soul. Try looking at things from other people's perspective. Put yourself in their shoes and ask yourself how you would feel or what choices you would make. If you're honest with yourself, you'll usually find that you can at least understand their actions, even if you don't agree with them.

Broader Scope Applications

The principles of Ma'at can be applied to your interactions with larger groups of people and society as a whole. You can set an example for others to follow by upholding these ideals in a position of leadership. It isn't always easy to act objectively, especially when there are people you don't like personally. However, you can't show favoritism. If you're a manager at a company, employees who do their work and follow the rules should be treated the same whether they're very friendly and personable or an unpleasant loner. Rewards need to be distributed to those who earn it, regardless of how you feel. There might be an employee you really like, but if someone else is a better fit for a promotion, it would go against the principles of Ma'at to give the position to the likable employee.

You can't limit your adherence to truth, justice, order, and balance to your own social network. If you see someone being wronged out in public, you should take action. Don't ignore a person who needs help. Stand up for someone who's getting bullied. Step in to tell the truth when you hear lies being spewed. Speak out against injustices, even if you aren't personally affected by them. As the saying goes, "The only thing necessary for the triumph of evil is for good men to do nothing." The fight against inequality, corruption, and immorality never ends. Isfet and Set are forever trying to sway people from the path of Ma'at. The forces of chaos and disorder never rest, so neither can you.

Practical Exercises

The wisdom of Ancient Egypt is just as applicable now as it was then. Take some time to reflect on the principles of Ma'at and consider how they apply to your life. There are always ways you can improve your devotion to truth, justice, order, and balance. Complete the following exercises to help you prove your worthiness when the time of your final judgment arrives:

Daily Affirmations to Connect with Ma'at

For this exercise, you will choose 7 of the Declarations of Innocence that can apply to your own life. You will also need a daily journal. Each morning, recite one of those affirmations out loud as your intention for the day. Record that day's declaration in your journal, and take it with you wherever you go. Throughout the day, jot down any interactions you have, decisions you make, and significant events that occur. Do your best to stay true to your declarations. In the evenings, read over your journal and reflect on whether or not you managed to uphold the Laws of Ma'at. Write down your conclusions in that day's entry.

After a week, you will have made all 7 declarations. When you look back at the week and read over everything you recorded in your journal, you'll be able to recognize certain patterns of behavior. You should analyze those patterns and determine what you need to change in order to better adhere to the principles of Ma'at. If you feel like this exercise is beneficial, do it again the next week, choosing 7 new Declarations of Innocence to affirm. You can even continue the exercise for a total of 6 weeks, after which you will have completed all 42 Declarations of Innocence, just like the departed souls must do in the Hall of Truth to prove they are worthy of A'aru.

Chant of Empowerment for Balance

This is a chant to empower you in the principles of Ma'at. You can use it during moments of emotional or spiritual imbalance to get you back on the right path. Make your intention clear by holding a feather to symbolize your connection to Ma'at. Speak with a steady voice when reciting the following chant:

I walk in Ma'at. I breathe in Ma'at.
Truth before me, harmony behind me.
Justice to my left, compassion to my right.
In the center I stand firm, unbowed, unbroken.

Sky above, ground below,
Between them I rise, rooted in honor.
My heart is light, my words ring true,
My will is focused – there is no fear.
Oh Ma'at, Goddess of Balance,
Make strong my steps and calm my storm.
Let chaos fall away like dust,
Let peace and purpose thrive.
As the sun shines and the Earth turns,
As the Nile ebbs and flows,
I claim my place, I claim my power.
I am balanced. I endure. I rise.
My heart is light, my soul is pure,
No evil shall endure.
So it is. So it shall be.
I walk in Ma'at. Ma'at walks in me.

Ethical Decision-Making Exercise

This exercise will help you ensure your choices follow the principles of Ma'at. Start by identifying a decision you need to make. It can be anything, no matter how big or small, like the way you choose to interact with a friend, what to do with a wallet you find on the ground, or deciding if you want to divorce your spouse. Ask yourself whether or not this choice aligns with truth and fairness and if it contributes to harmony or creates discord.

Were you dismissive of your friend when they tried to talk to you about something, or did you listen to what they had to say? Did you try to find the owner of the wallet, or were you tempted to take the money in it and toss it back on the ground? Are you considering leaving your spouse after doing your best to work out your problems, or are you acting impulsively on your emotions after they hurt you?

It's not always easy to find the right answer. With some decisions, the path that follows the principles of Ma'at is obvious, like returning the wallet to its owner without taking anything from it. However, other situations aren't always as cut and dry. Decisions that will have a major effect on your life need to be carefully considered before you act on them. When you're confused or uncertain about the correct course of action, you can call upon Ma'at to help you gain more insight and understanding of your choices. Meditate to clear your mind and recite the following invocation:

> *Dua Ma'at, Goddess of Balance,*
> *Feather of Truth upon the scales of the heart,*
> *You who ordered the stars and give voice to rightness,*
> *I call upon you now.*
> *A choice now stands before me,*
> *A path that forks in opposite directions*
> *Leading me to an uncertain future,*
> *And I would not walk either path blindly.*
> *I seek not comfort, but truth.*
> *I seek not power, but righteousness.*
> *I seek to act in harmony with the way of things,*
> *And stay true to your ideals.*
> *Come into my heart, Oh Ma'at,*
> *Make it light and clear.*
> *Strip away my fear, my pride, my doubt.*
> *Leave only what serves the balance.*
> *What will honor the sacred order?*
> *What brings no harm where harm is not due?*
> *What preserves that which is just,*
> *Even if it shall cost me dearly?*
> *Let my thoughts be measured.*
> *Let my words be weighed.*
> *Let my actions reflect your divine law.*
> *Oh great Ma'at, guide my feet.*
> *Let no lie pass my lips.*
> *Let no selfishness cloud my sight.*
> *Let the choice I make ripple in truth,*
> *Not only for me, but for all it touches.*
> *So I invoke you, Feather of the Sky,*
> *Daughter of Ra, She Who Rises with the Sun.*

Walk with me. Speak through me.
And let Ma'at endure through my choice.
Dua Ma'at. Dua Ma'at. Dua Ma'at.

When you have finished your invocation, write down the possible outcomes of your decision. Make sure to consider all angles and try to view things from the other side. Take your time when weighing your options. Finally, choose the path that feels most balanced and ethical, that feels like it honors the ideals of Ma'at.

Ritual of Truth (Self-Reflection)

To complete the Ritual of Truth exercise, sit quietly with a feather that represents Ma'at and reflect on your day. Ask yourself: *"Have I spoken and acted in truth? Have I upheld balance in my life and with others?"*

Write down any imbalances or mistakes you can think of, and then place the feather on top of the page. Visualize silver threads of energy coming out of the words you wrote and entering the feather. Feel yourself releasing your faults and imperfections into the feather. When you're finished, you will symbolically let them go by placing the feather on your altar and reciting a brief prayer. You can also go outside under the stars and place the feather on a stone, tree stump, or hillock. Close your eyes and repeat the following:

"Hear me, Ma'at – I speak to the arbiter of justice and truth. I am flawed, but I am human. My mistakes do not define me. I give you my burdens and cast them away. With your blessings, I have brought my heart into balance once more."

You can then burn or bury the feather. Dig a hole in the earth with your hands, place the feather or its ashes inside, and cover it back up. Show your gratitude to Ma'at by working to uphold her ideals.

Community Service with Ma'at

A great way to prove your devotion to the principles of Ma'at is to volunteer for a cause that promotes justice, balance or environmental sustainability. Acknowledge that Ma'at is the inspiration for your actions by dedicating your service to her. Before doing any volunteer work, speak the following recitation:

Dua Ma'at, She of the Feather and the Scales,
Lady of Rightness, Guide of Hearts,
I offer this work, this act of service,

As a living reflection of your order.
May my hands bring balance,
May my words carry truth,
May my presence bring peace,
Wherever there is need.
I serve not for praise, but for harmony.
I give not for glory, but for justice.
Let this deed uphold your name,
Let this moment be woven into the fabric of Ma'at.
So may it be. So may it endure.
Dua Ma'at.

When you have finished your volunteer work, recite the following:

Dua Ma'at, Lady of the Just Heart,
Mistress of the Scale of Two Lands,
The deed is done, the offering made.
I give thanks for the strength to serve,
For the chance to restore balance,
Even if only in small ways.
If I have eased a single burden,
And made another's life a little better,
It is a gift for which I am grateful,
Let this service ripple outward,
Touching what I cannot see,
Guided by your eternal law.
As I return to my daily routine,
May Ma'at remain in my breath,
In my choices, and in my heart.
May balance be upheld.
May I walk in your light, always.
Dua Ma'at. May truth endure.

Chapter 9: Preserving Kemetic Wisdom for the Future

Kemetism is such a rich and complex religion that it can take years to learn everything it has to offer. If you join a Kemetic temple, there's even more to discover. Each branch of Kemetism has its own approach to the various spiritual, theological, and practical aspects of the religion, as well as certain idiosyncrasies that set it apart from the others. However, at their core, they all share the same foundation in Ancient Egyptian beliefs and the same goal of preserving those beliefs for future generations.

Preservation of Beliefs

When compared to other neopagan religions, such as Wicca, Celtic Revival, Neo-Druidism, Roman Traditionalism, and Asatru, Kemetism is still relatively new. In order to survive, it needs to spread its message and faith to all corners of the globe. It isn't just about the continuation of Kemetism, though – it's about keeping the traditions of the Ancient Egyptian religion alive. While the knowledge of Ancient Egypt isn't likely to disappear anytime soon, there's a big difference between reading about the Neteru, heka, and maat, and actually experiencing what it's like to practice those beliefs. The world would be a poorer place if the Kemetic invocations, symbols of power, and hieroglyphic spells were relegated to the annals of history.

Knowledge from the Past

The only reason Kemetism exists today is because the wisdom and knowledge of the Ancient Egyptians were well-preserved over the ages. When archeologists and Egyptologists uncovered cities, temples, pyramids, tombs, and other structures, they found written records of Ancient Egypt's history, beliefs, customs, and mythology. Although they dug up items of gold and precious stones, the real treasures were the scrolls, books, and hieroglyphic writings that gave us a glimpse into the world of Ancient Egypt 3,000 years ago.

Temple of Isis, Aswan, Egypt.[88]

There were also pieces of information about the lost kingdoms of the pharaohs provided by sources from other contemporary cultures. The Greeks and Romans, in particular, were fascinated by the Ancient Egyptians and even attempted to incorporate some Ancient Egyptian lore into their own mythology, such as correlating their gods with the likes of Ra, Horus, Osiris, Anubis, Isis, Hathor, Amun, and the rest of the pantheon. Kemetism has reconstructed much of what the Ancient Egyptians practiced and took cues from other religions of the ancient world to fill in the rest.

In a way, things have come full circle. Ancient pagans were influenced by Ancient Egyptians, and modern Kemetism is influenced by those ancient pagans. It's fitting, really – the cycle keeps going, just as the Ancient Egyptians believed. It now falls to Kemetic enthusiasts and practitioners to help preserve all that knowledge and wisdom for the dawn of the next cycle.

Lessons for the Present

With all the chaos and injustice plaguing the modern world, it can be easy to forget that what we're experiencing isn't unique. There have been many points throughout history where those living through those times felt like the world was on the brink of total annihilation: the fall of Rome, the Black Death, the Thirty Years' War, the Year Without a Summer, and both World Wars. Looking back, things don't seem as grim since we know how it all played out. However, when you're in the midst of a global crisis, uncertainty about the future is understandable.

One way to stay grounded and avoid giving in to despair is to embrace a religion like Kemetism. It can offer comfort and guidance, helping you to tap into your spirituality. Humanity might succumb to greed, corruption, and hatred, leaving you feeling disappointed in your fellow man, but the Neteru will never let you down. They exist in their most perfect form as divine beings who are both gods and concepts. Even the deities that represent negative aspects, like Isfet and Set, succeed in performing their role in the cosmic balance.

Without darkness, there can be no light. Without chaos, there can be no order. Without lies, there can be no truth. Without villains, there can be no heroes. Everything in the myths and legends is balanced. They are like a roadmap that leads to salvation. The gods, stories, and traditions show you an example of things going wrong in order to teach you how to make them right again. Set murdered Osiris and usurped the throne, but eventually, Horus defeated him and reclaimed it. Isis even managed to resurrect her husband, transforming him into more than what he was. We must all go through a transformation if we wish to become a better version of ourselves.

The Neteru are there for you throughout all stages of your life. As you change and grow, different gods will naturally align with your experiences. Thoth, the god of wisdom and knowledge, makes for the perfect deity when you're going through school and college. Hathor, the goddess of love and joy, is who you'd want by your side when embarking on a new relationship. Isis was fiercely protective of her son, which is very relatable to anyone who becomes a parent. Bes watches over households, something that would bring comfort to those with families. When you reach retirement age, Horus will keep you safe. As you move ever closer to the end, Osiris can offer reassurance that you will be reborn in the afterlife.

Painting of the Neteru from an Egyptian Tomb.⁵⁴

Staying true to the Kemetic ideals of honesty, justice, fairness, and balance can help you lead an honorable and fulfilling life. If you start to stray from the path, the gods will be there to guide you back. Remember to slow down and reflect on your actions, decisions, and relationships, evaluating your adherence to the principles of Ma'at. The Neteru are all around you, whether in their form as gods or as natural forces. You can find evidence of their sacred power in the little moments, like the taste of a good home-cooked meal or the scent of wildflowers while hiking through the woods. Make sure you show the gods your gratitude for everything they provide.

Wisdom for the Future

Nobody can say for certain what the future will bring. All throughout history, many have tried to predict it with mixed results. They're not so much predictions as they are educated guesses. Right now, you might be entirely devoted to Kemetism, but that doesn't mean things can't change down the line. Everyone responds to major upheaval in their lives differently. Suffering a loss or tragedy can significantly reshape your worldview. When that happens, it can be perfectly natural to experience doubt or question your beliefs.

There's no shame in feeling lost or confused. Your spiritual journey will likely hit at least a few bumps in the road. If that happens, you can always look back at how far you've come. Remember who you were before you became involved in Kemetism. Think about the lessons it taught you, the comfort it offered, and the benefits you enjoyed. Reflect on your spiritual growth and how strong you felt when your life was at its best. Things might be bad now, but they'll get better again. Everything is a cycle.

Knowing that tomorrow could be better than today should be an encouraging thought.

The best part of any religion is its community. Whether you belong to a temple that has large ceremonial gatherings or mostly practice Kemetism on your own, there are many others out there doing the same thing. You can contact them in person or reach out to them over the Internet. Your fellow practitioners understand what you're experiencing with your beliefs, whether it's good or bad. They can help you grow stronger in your faith and teach you more about the religion. Someday, you can do the same for those just starting out on their journey.

Passing along wisdom and knowledge is how Kemetism will stay alive. It's how you can do your part to preserve the customs and traditions for the future. With everything you've learned after reading this book, you're well on your way to fulfilling that goal. Share your beliefs with the people in your life. Encourage them to check it out. You know what it's like exploring Kemetism in the beginning, so offer them some guidance. For the time being, you should feel proud that you've taken your first steps into the world of Kemetism. When the day comes to have your heart weight in the Hall of Truth, you can look back and see that today started you on the path to being deemed worthy of eternal paradise.

Practical Exercises

This book is nearly at its close, but your education in Kemetism never really ends. If you keep an open mind and a faithful heart, you will continue to learn and grow. We'll leave you with a few more exercises to help you along in your spiritual journey:

Daily Kemetic Routine

For this exercise, you'll be creating your own daily routine for honoring the gods and upholding the values of Kemetism. You should choose whatever type of magic or spirituality that resonates with you. For example, you could start with morning affirmations of Ma'at, vowing to act with integrity and balance throughout the day. After waking up, recite the following:

"I rise with the light of Ma'at in my heart, grounded in truth, clarity, and balance. Today, I walk in harmony with the world, speaking only what is just and doing only what is right."

At lunchtime, you could give thanks to the Neteru and ask them to bless your meal. Just speak the following words:

"Dua Neteru, divine ones of light and life, I thank you for this meal. I am grateful for the hands that prepared it and the blessings that made it possible. May this food nourish my body, strengthen my spirit, and help me walk in step with Ma'at."

If you like to take an afternoon stroll through the park, you could chant a spell to protect your legs from cramping up. Try a chant like this one:

"By the strength of Horus and the grace of Sekhmet, let my legs move freely and without pain. As I walk through this world in devotion to the Neteru, may no cramp or burden slow my steps."

Finally, in the evening, you could invoke Thoth when helping your children with their homework. All you have to do is repeat the following:

"Oh Thoth, God of Wisdom and Divine Scribe, please grant me patience and clarity of mind, that I may guide my child with understanding. Let your knowledge flow through us both, lighting the path of knowledge with your sacred wisdom."

Create Your Kemetic Library

You can start compiling your own Kemetic library to have all the information you learn at your fingertips and possibly share it with others interested in Kemetism. Your personal collection can consist of texts, symbols, and tools that encompass the breadth of your knowledge. Gather anything related to Kemetism, such as books, journals, spells, illustrations of hieroglyphs, and small objects like candles, statues, and ritual items. Pick a dedicated space to store your collection and organize your materials however you want. You can catalog them by type, by subject, by individual Neteru, or alphabetically. Treat your library as a sacred resource for study, reflection, and inspiration. If you ever have children, you can pass it on to them to help preserve Kemetism for the future.

Write Your Kemetic Creed

It's time to reflect on everything you've learned and write a personal statement – a creed – that encapsulates your religious intentions and spiritual connection to Kemetic beliefs. Your creed can be in the form of an affirmation, such as:

"I walk in Ma'at, honoring truth and balance. I carry the power of Heka, shaping my reality in alignment with the divine."

Your creed can be more of a mission statement, saying something like:

"I will follow the principles of Ma'at and live my life in accordance with truth, justice, order, and balance."

If you want to structure your creed more like a recitation, it can affirm your spiritual journey and devotion to the ideals of Ma'at and the Neteru. Try something like this:

I honor the Neteru, the divine forces who shape all things.

I offer gratitude to Ra, who rises with the sun and renews the world.

I recall the lessons of Osiris, who died and was reborn.

I follow the example of Isis, who is unrivaled in the power of heka.

I carry the protection of Horus, ever watchful and ever strong.

I speak with the wisdom of Thoth, truthful and concise.

I act with the compassion of Sekhmet and the grace of Hathor.

I serve my ancestors with love, and I know they walk beside me.

I tend the gardens of our sacred Earth, preserving it for the future.

I strive for justice, live in peace, and work to restore harmony.

I make offerings not only with my hands but with my heart and deeds.

I am a child of Ma'at, and through her, I endure and rise.

Don't worry – you don't have to make the perfect creed right out of the gate. You can revisit and refine it periodically as your faith evolves. What matters is that you reflect on what you want to get out of your spiritual journey and what your beliefs mean to you. Your relationship with Kemetism is a very personal experience. As long as you hold true to your values, you can't go wrong.

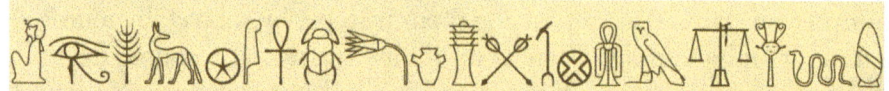

Appendix: Kemetic Magic Glossary

This book has many words and concepts that are unfamiliar to the uninitiated. Here's a glossary of words related to Kemetic magic to give you a reminder:

Term	Definition	Hieroglyph
A'aru	Field of Reeds; Ancient Egyptian afterlife paradise	
Akh	Reunited spirit of the deceased	
Akhet	Season of Inundation (July to October)	
Altar	A dedicated sacred space dedicated to the gods and used to perform rituals	
Amun	God of Air and Sky	
Ankh	Symbol of life	

Term	Definition	Hieroglyph
Anubis	God of Mummification and the Afterlife	
Atum	Creator God	
Ba	Essence and individuality of a deceased spirit; part of the Akh	
Bastet	Goddess of Cats, Fertility, and Women	
Benben	A mound that rose from the primordial waters	
Bes	Goddess Joy, Childbirth, and Protection	
Devotional	An incantation used regularly to express your commitment to the gods	
Djed Pillar	Symbol of Osiris, God of the Dead and Afterlife	
Dua	The act of praise, worship, or adoration	
Duat	Ancient Egyptian underworld	

Term	Definition	Hieroglyph
El	Ancient Egyptian word for earth	
Ennead	Group of nine deities from the Heliopolis creation myth	
Hall of Truth	Location in the Duat where the Weighing of the Heart ritual takes place; home of the 42 Assessors of Ma'at	
Hathor	Goddess of Love, Marriage, and Fertility	
Heka	Magic; God of Magic and Medicine	
Horus	God of Kingship and Protection	
Ib	The heart; part of the Akh	
Iconomancy	Practice of using representations of the gods for rituals and spells	
Incense	Organic substance that gives off smoke and aroma when burned; used for rituals and cleansings	
Invocation	An incantation used during rituals to call or summon the gods	

Term	Definition	Hieroglyph
Ka	The vital life force of a deceased spirit, part of the Akh	
Ka	Ancient Egyptian word for fire	
Kemet	Name of Ancient Egypt	
Khet	The corpse of a deceased soul, part of the Akh	
Leem	Ancient Egyptian word for water	
Maat	Balance; Goddess of Truth, Justice, and Balance	
Mandjet	Solar barque used by Ra to take the sun across the sky	
Mesektet	Lunar barque used by Ra to take the sun through the underworld	
Nephthys	Goddess of Decay, Mourning, and Magic	
Neteru (Neter)	The pantheon of Ancient Egyptian and Kemetic gods and goddesses	
Nu	Primordial waters of chaos from before the universe was created; deity who is the personification of chaos	

Term	Definition	Hieroglyph
Offering	Food, drink, flower, symbol, or item given as a gift to the gods	
Ogdoad	Group of eight deities from the Thebes and Hermopolis creation myths	
Om	Ancient Egyptian word for air	
Oneiromancy	The practice of interpreting dreams for guidance and divination; dreamwork	
Peret	Season of Emergence (November to February)	
Pharaoh	Title of the Ancient Egyptian monarch	
Ptah	God of Craftsmen and Artisans	
Ra	God of the Sun	
Ren	A person's name; part of the Akh	
Sah	The spiritual body of a deceased soul, part of the Akh	

Term	Definition	Hieroglyph
Scarab	Symbol of Khepri, God of Rebirth and Transformation	
Sekhem	A person's power; part of the Akh	
Set	God of Chaos and Violence	
Shemu	Season of Harvest (March to June	
Shuyet	A person's shadow; part of the Akh	
Sistrum	Ancient Egyptian instrument connected to the gods	
Thoth	God of Wisdom and Knowledge	
Tyet Knot	Symbol of Isis, Goddess of Healing and Magic	
Uraeus	The symbol of royal authority of gods and pharaohs	
Was-Scepter	Symbol of power and dominion	

If you enjoyed this book, I'd greatly appreciate a review on Amazon because it helps me to create more books that people want. It would mean a lot to hear from you.

To leave a review:
1. Open your camera app.
2. Point your mobile device at the QR code.
3. The review page will appear in your web browser.

Thanks for your support!

Here's another book by Mari Silva that you might like

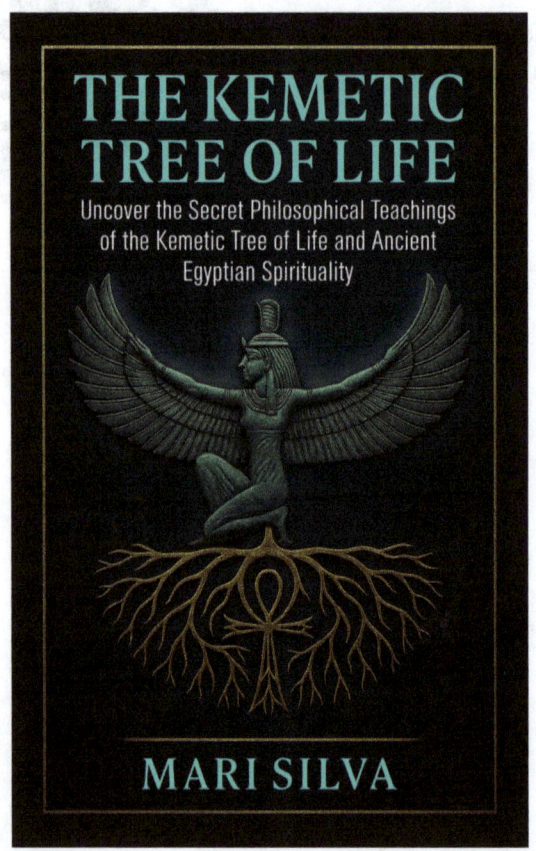

Your Free Gift
(only available for a limited time)

Thanks for getting this book! If you want to learn more about various spirituality topics, then join Mari Silva's community and get a free guided meditation MP3 for awakening your third eye. This guided meditation mp3 is designed to open and strengthen ones third eye so you can experience a higher state of consciousness. Simply visit the link below the image to get started.

https://spiritualityspot.com/meditation

Or, Scan the QR code!

References

Abdalla, S. (2023, December 21). *The Ancient Egyptian View of the Human Psyche – the Ka, the Ba, and the Akh*. CSA Reviving Community. https://csa-living.org/oasis-blog/the-ancient-egyptian-view-of-the-human-psyche-the-ka-the-ba-and-the-akh

Aloe and More. (2025). *History Of Aloe*. Aloeandmore.co.uk. https://www.aloeandmore.co.uk/history-of-aloe?srsltid=AfmBOop98KKLe7seBLoJ8Ry7Vv8cQRmpW9bLcylaVX57UY6_u9x5qsEJ

Aly, & Hussien. (2025). *EGYPTIAN CHAMOMILE - CULTIVATION & INDUSTRIAL PROCESSING*. Actahort.org. https://www.actahort.org/books/749/749_6.htm

Assmann, J. (2001). *The search for God in ancient Egypt*. Cornell University Press.

Assmann, J. (2005). *Death and salvation in ancient Egypt*. Cornell University Press.

Assmann, J., & Livingstone, R. (2006). *Religion and cultural memory: ten studies*. Stanford University Press.

Barta, M. (2020). *Bárta, M. Abusir and its place in the history of ancient Egyptian civilization, in M. Bárta, ed. Kings of the Sun. Studies.* Kings of the Sun. Studies. https://www.academia.edu/48831598/B%C3%A1rta_M_Abusir_and_its_place_in_the_history_of_ancient_Egyptian_civilisation_in_M_B%C3%A1rta_ed_Kings_of_the_Sun_Studies

Bertol, E., Fineschi, V., Karch, S. B., Mari, F., & Riezzo, I. (2004). Nymphaea cults in ancient Egypt and the New World: a lesson in empirical pharmacology. *JRSM, 97*(2), 84-85. https://doi.org/10.1258/jrsm.97.2.84

Bleeker, C. J. (1973). The Cult of Thoth. *BRILL EBooks, 26*, 151-155. https://doi.org/10.1163/9789004378445_008

Budge, E. A. W. (1895). *The Egyptian Book of the Dead Index*. Www.sacred-Texts.com. https://www.sacred-texts.com/egy/ebod/index.htm

Cassar, C. (2024, January 31). *The 42 Laws of Maat: The Moral Principles of the Ancient Egyptians*. Anthropology Review. https://anthropologyreview.org/history/ancient-egypt/42-laws-of-maat-principles/

Contributors, W. E. (2024, June 3). *Health Benefits of Frankincense Essential Oil*. WebMD. https://www.webmd.com/diet/health-benefits-frankincense-essential-oil

Cresswell, B. (2021). *Your Healing Voice. An Introduction to Toning through Humming*. Academyofsoundhealing.com. https://www.academyofsoundhealing.com/blog/your-healing-voice-an-introduction-to-toning

Cronkleton, E. (2017, October 6). *Holotropic Breathwork: Usage, Safety, and More*. Healthline. https://www.healthline.com/health/holotropic-breathwork

CSA Living. (2023, December 14). *The Protective Qualities of Garlic: From Ancient Egyptian Magical Rituals to Modern-day Sustainable Pesticide*. CSA Reviving Community. https://csa-living.org/oasis-blog/the-protective-qualities-of-garlicnbspfrom-ancient-egyptian-magical-rituals-to-modern-day-sustainable-pesticide

Daugherty, M. (2014, October 2). *Kemetism – Ancient Religions in our Modern World*. Archaeology of Ancient Egypt. https://web.archive.org/web/20180228030246/http://anthropology.msu.edu/anp455-fs14/2014/10/02/kemetism-ancient-religions-in-our-modern-world/

David, R. (2002). *Religion and Magic in Ancient Egypt*. Penguin UK.

Davidson, K. (2020, September 25). *Blue Lotus Flower: Uses, Benefits, and Safety*. Healthline. https://www.healthline.com/nutrition/blue-lotus-flower

DevoTTR. (2012, May 30). *Kemetic Priesthood: Then and Now*. The Twisted Rope. https://thetwistedrope.wordpress.com/2012/05/30/kemetic-priesthood-then-and-now/

Dienstmann, G. (2015, May 26). *How to Deepen Your Meditation to Achieve Altered States of Consciousness | HighExistence*. HighExistence | Explore Life's Deepest Questions; HighExistence | Explore Life's Deepest Questions. https://www.highexistence.com/how-to-deepen-your-mediation-process/

Dioreo, P. (2025). *Sacred Geometry*. Mit.edu. https://web.mit.edu/4.299/Students/diop/intro.html

Egyptian History. (2020, December 7). *WAS SCEPTRE*. Egyptian History. https://egyptian-history.com/blogs/egyptian-symbols/was-scepter

Elkins, G. R., & Olendzki, N. (2018). *Mindful Hypnotherapy*. Springer Publishing Company.

Farr, K. (2015, May 28). *The History of Thyme | Myspicer | Wholesale Spices & Herbs*. MySpicer | Spices, Herbs, Seasonings. https://www.myspicer.com/the-history-of-thyme/

Felman, A. (2018, August 23). *Thyme: Benefits, History, and Forms*. Www.medicalnewstoday.com. https://www.medicalnewstoday.com/articles/266016

Forrest, M. I. (2022, December 25). *Making Offering to Isis*. Isiopolis. https://isiopolis.com/2022/12/25/making-offering-to-isis-2/

Françoise Dunand, & Zivie-Coche, C. (2004). *Gods and men in Egypt: 3000 BCE to 395 CE*. Cornell University Press.

Frankfurter, D. (1998). *Religion in Roman Egypt: Assimilation and Resistance*. Princeton Univ. Press.

Gavin, P. (2023, May 10). *The Ancient Wonders of Fennel*. Tablet Magazine. https://www.tabletmag.com/sections/food/articles/ancient-wonders-fennel

Gorringe, H. (1882). *Egyptian Obelisks*. Google Books. https://books.google.com/books?id=Gf4-AQAAMAAJ&printsec=frontcover&source=gbs_ge_summary_r&cad=0#v=onepage&q&f=false

Haadi, A. (2014, August 27). *Materials, Plants and Tools used in Heka and Egyptian Magic*. Egyptian Witchcraft. https://www.egyptian-witchcraft.com/materials-plants-and-tools/

Harrison, P. (2017). *Profane Egyptologists*. Routledge.

Hart, G. (1990). *Egyptian myths: Hart, George: Free Download, Borrow, and Streaming: Internet Archive*. Internet Archive. https://archive.org/details/egyptianmyths00hart/page/8/mode/2up

Hart, G. (2005). *The Routledge Dictionary of Egyptian Gods and Goddesses*. Routledge.

Hill, J. (2008). *Maat | Ancient Egypt Online*. Ancient Egypt Online. https://ancientegyptonline.co.uk/maat/

Holland, T., & Schoen, R. (2008). *The Mechanics of Ancient Egypt Magical Practice*. https://isac.uchicago.edu/sites/default/files/uploads/shared/docs/saoc54_4th.pdf

Hornung, E. (2001). *The secret lore of Egypt: its impact on the West*. Cornell University Press.

James Peter Allen. (2000). *Middle Egyptian: an introduction to the language and culture of hieroglyphs*. Cambridge University Press.

Jolly Lane Greenhouse. (2023). *The Healing History of Aloe Vera Plants: An Ancient Plant with Modern Uses*. Jollylane.com.

https://www.jollylane.com/growing-tips/article/the-healing-history-of-aloe-vera-plants-an-ancient-plants-with-modern-uses/

Katja Goebs. (2010, November 9). *Crowns (Egyptian)*. Academia.edu. https://www.academia.edu/364686/Crowns_Egyptian_

Kemet. (2019, February 25). *Ancient Egypt Mythology*. Kemet Experience. https://www.kemetexperience.com/ancient-egypt-mythology/

Kemet Experience. (2019, March 24). *The 42 ideals of Ma'at*. Kemet Experience. https://www.kemetexperience.com/the-42-ideals-of-maat/

Khan, A. (2024, September 13). *The Historical Uses of Fennel Seeds*. Chikka Chikka Shop. https://chikkachikka.com/blogs/news/the-historical-uses-of-fennel-seeds

Klimczak, N. (2016, September 17). *The Magic of Heka: Ancient Egyptian Rituals That Have Crossed Cultures and Time*. Ancient-Origins.net; Ancient Origins. https://www.ancient-origins.net/history-ancient-traditions/magic-heka-ancient-egyptian-rituals-have-crossed-cultures-and-time-006668

Licorice International. (2025). *About Licorice*. Licorice International. https://licoriceinternational.com/pages/about-licorice?srsltid=AfmBOoo3ouiUv7foZYOnHQ8L3QV_pEho_WIYJzB1jHM5qBOHYPlM7ICx

Mark, J. J. (2017a, February 24). *Magic in Ancient Egypt*. World History Encyclopedia. https://www.worldhistory.org/article/1019/magic-in-ancient-egypt/

Mark, J. J. (2017b, March 2). *The Soul in Ancient Egypt*. World History Encyclopedia. https://www.worldhistory.org/article/1023/the-soul-in-ancient-egypt/

Martin, D. (2008). Maat and Order in African Cosmology: A Conceptual Tool for Understanding Indigenous Knowledge. *Journal of Black Studies, 38*(6), 951–967. https://www.jstor.org/stable/40035033

McCracken, E. (2024, June 15). *The History of Liquorice: From Ancient Remedies to Modern Sweets - Saint Valentines Liquorice Company*. Saint Valentine's Liquorice Company. https://valentines-liquorice.uk/the-history-of-liquorice-from-ancient-remedies-to-modern-sweets/

McKinnon, H. L., & Hamada, K. (2022, October 14). Why Is Chamomile Suddenly Everywhere? *The New York Times*. https://www.nytimes.com/2022/10/14/t-magazine/chamomile-food-fashion.html

Menu, B. (1987). *L'obélisque de la Concorde*. Librairie Orientaliste Paul Geuthner.

Metropolitan Museum of Art. (2019). *Heart Scarab of Hatnefer*. Metmuseum.org. https://www.metmuseum.org/art/collection/search/545146

Metropolitan Museum of Art. (2020). *Girdle of Isis (Tyet Knot)*. Metmuseum.org. https://www.metmuseum.org/art/collection/search/548207

Metropolitan Museum of Art. (2022). *Letter written in hieratic script on papyrus.* Metmuseum.org. https://www.metmuseum.org/art/collection/search/544847

Metropolitan Museum of Art. (2024). *Lamp | The Metropolitan Museum of Art.* The Metropolitan Museum of Art. https://www.metmuseum.org/art/collection/search/444791

Miller, M. D. (2020). *Egyptian Sacred Geometry: Shape Has Power. The ancient Egyptians knew how to capture positive, beneficial energies from the Universe. Learn their secrets to harness these energies to improve your life.*

Moroney, M. (2023). *Egyptian Jewelry: A Window into Ancient Culture.* American Research Center in Egypt. https://arce.org/resource/egyptian-jewelry-window-ancient-culture/

Picture This. (2024). *Unraveling the Mystical Charm and Significance of Roman Chamomile.* PictureThis. https://www.picturethisai.com/language-flower/Chamaemelum_nobile.html

Pinch, G. (2002). *Egyptian mythology: a guide to the gods, goddesses, and traditions of ancient Egypt.* Oxford University Press.

Poklis, J. L., Mulder, H. A., Halquist, M. S., Wolf, C. E., Poklis, A., & Peace, M. R. (2017). The Blue Lotus Flower (Nymphea caerulea) Resin Used in a New Type of Electronic Cigarette, the Re-Buildable Dripping Atomizer. *Journal of Psychoactive Drugs, 49*(3), 175–181. https://doi.org/10.1080/02791072.2017.1290304

Republic of Tea. (2019). *Herbal Folklore: Myths & Legends About Herbs | The Republic of Tea.* Republicoftea.com. https://www.republicoftea.com/blog/tea-library/herbal-folklore-myths-legends-about-herbs/tl-028/

Sciortino, P. (2025). *Learn Hieroglyphs.* Hieroglyphs.net. http://hieroglyphs.net/cgi/pager.pl?p=01

Serpico, M. (2019). *Language and Literacy.* Ucl.ac.uk. https://www.ucl.ac.uk/3dpetriemuseum/stories/ancient-life/egyptian-life/language-and-literacy.html

Sever, A. (2024, February 13). *Ptah, Egyptian God of Arts & Crafts: Offerings, Rituals..* Occultist. https://occultist.net/ptah-offerings-rituals-prayers-powers/

Shamanic Journey. (2015, February 15). *Shamanic Journey – Information on Shamanic Journeying, Shamans and Shamanism, includes information on Shamans Initiation, Plants used by Shamans and Trance Dance.* Shamanicjourney.com. https://www.shamanicjourney.com/

Short, M. (2010, January 21). *Offerings to Horus – Margret E. Short Fine Arts.* Margretshort.com. https://margretshort.com/offerings-to-horus/

Steele, P. (2009). *Ancient Egypt.* Rosen Pub.

Strudwick, H. (2006). *The Encyclopedia of Ancient Egypt.* Amber Books.

Taylor, R. (2000). *Death and the Afterlife: A Cultural Encyclopedia*. ABC-CLIO (Bloomsbury Publishing).

Team, E. (2024, December 3). *Ancient Egypt Priests and Their Sacred Role in Temple Life*. Egypt Tours Portal. https://www.egypttoursportal.com/blog/ancient-egyptian-civilization/ancient-egyptian-priests/

Teeter, E. (1998). Egyptian Warfare and Weapons. Ian ShawEgyptian Shabtis. Harry M. Stewart. *Journal of Near Eastern Studies, 57*(4), 299–300. https://doi.org/10.1086/468658

The House of Netjer. (2024). *Netjer | Kemet.org*. Kemet.org. https://www.kemet.org/taxonomy/term/123

The House of Netjer. (2025). *Kemet.org What is Kemetic Orthodoxy?* Archive.org. https://web.archive.org/web/20080911234223/http://www.kemet.org/kemexp1.html

Touwaide, A., & Appetiti, E. (2022). *Herbs in History: Fennel*. Ahpa.org. https://www.ahpa.org/herbs_in_history_fennel

u/AearaLaRose1332. (2023, June 4). *Blocked Page*. Reddit.com. https://www.reddit.com/r/Kemetic/comments/140cp79/comment/jmwp5f5/?utm_source=share&utm_medium=web3x&utm_name=web3xcss&utm_term=1&utm_content=share_button

u/WebenBanu. (2023, September 9). *Reddit - The heart of the internet*. Reddit.com. https://www.reddit.com/r/Kemetic/comments/16dypue/how_to_kemetic/

UC Master Gardeners of Butte County. (2025, March 31). *Herbs in History, Legend and Lore | UC Agriculture and Natural Resources*. UC Agriculture and Natural Resources. https://ucanr.edu/blog/real-dirt/article/herbs-history-legend-and-lore

University of South Florida. (2006). *The Egyptian Soul: the ka, the ba, and the akh*. Usf.edu. http://myweb.usf.edu/~liottan/theegyptiansoul.html

Wallis, A. (1899). *Egyptian Ideas Of The Future Life*. Jazzybee Verlag.

Warren, K. (2023). *Book of the Dead: A Guidebook to the Afterlife*. American Research Center in Egypt. https://arce.org/resource/book-dead-guidebook-afterlife/

Wilkinson, R. H. (1992). *Reading Egyptian art: a hieroglyphic guide to ancient Egyptian painting and sculpture*. Thames And Hudson.

Wilkinson, R. H. (2017). *The complete gods and goddesses of Ancient Egypt*. Thames & Hudson.

Yirser Ra Hotep. (2014, March 15). *Pose of Immortality - Yoga Chicago*. Yoga Chicago. https://yogachicago.com/2014/03/pose-of-immortality/

Image Sources

1 Designed by macrovector on Freepik. https://www.freepik.com/free-vector/cleopatra-flat-collage-with-pharaoh-figure-egyptian-gods-cultural-items-color-vector-illustration_34379307.htm#fromView=search&page=1&position=8&uuid=531f9ce2-e067-4576-9bf3-7b9f78ab3119&query=ancient+Egyptian+society

2 PharaohCrab, CC0, via Wikimedia Commons https://commons.wikimedia.org/wiki/File:Heka_god.svg

3 No machine-readable author provided. Jeff Dahl assumed (based on copyright claims)., CC BY-SA 4.0 <https://creativecommons.org/licenses/by-sa/4.0>, via Wikimedia Commons https://commons.wikimedia.org/wiki/File:Maat.svg

4 Jeff Dahl, CC BY-SA 4.0 <https://creativecommons.org/licenses/by-sa/4.0>, via Wikimedia Commons https://commons.wikimedia.org/wiki/File:Crook_and_flail.svg

5 Metropolitan Museum of Art, CC0, via Wikimedia Commons https://commons.wikimedia.org/wiki/File:Heart_Scarab_of_Hatnefer_MET_36.3.2_EGDP013730.jpg

6 Ruth Hartnup, Attribution 2.0 Generic, CC BY 2.0 <https://creativecommons.org/licenses/by/2.0/deed.en> https://www.flickr.com/photos/ruthanddave/264056202

7 Jeff Dahl, CC BY-SA 4.0 <https://creativecommons.org/licenses/by-sa/4.0>, via Wikimedia Commons, https://commons.wikimedia.org/wiki/File:Imiut_fetish.svg

8 https://commons.wikimedia.org/wiki/File:C%2BB-Music-Fig5-EgyptianSistrum.PNG

9 বিশ্বজিৎ বৈশ্য, CC BY-SA 4.0 <https://creativecommons.org/licenses/by-sa/4.0>, via Wikimedia Commons https://commons.wikimedia.org/wiki/File:A_Burning_Clay_Lamp_in_Assam.jpg

10 PharaohCrab, CC0, via Wikimedia Commons, https://commons.wikimedia.org/wiki/File:Nemes.svg

11 Jeff Dahl, CC BY-SA 4.0 <https://creativecommons.org/licenses/by-sa/4.0>, via Wikimedia Commons https://commons.wikimedia.org/wiki/File:Eye_of_Horus_bw.svg

12 Metropolitan Museum of Art, CC0, via Wikimedia Commons https://commons.wikimedia.org/wiki/File:Tit_(Isis_knot)_amulet_MET_DP109370.jpg

13 Rama, CC BY-SA 3.0 FR <https://creativecommons.org/licenses/by-sa/3.0/fr/deed.en>, via Wikimedia Commons, https://commons.wikimedia.org/wiki/File:Ramesses_IV-N_438-IMG_8065-gradient.jpg

14 Mary Harrsch, Attribution-NonCommercial-ShareAlike 2.0 Generic, CC BY-NC-SA 2.0 <https://creativecommons.org/licenses/by-nc-sa/2.0/deed.en> https://www.flickr.com/photos/mharrsch/22106320673

15 Wally Gobetz, Attribution-NonCommercial-NoDerivs 2.0 Generic, CC BY-NC-ND 2.0 < https://creativecommons.org/licenses/by-nc-nd/2.0/deed.en> https://www.flickr.com/photos/wallyg/54209570294

16 Alexi Helligar, CC BY-SA 3.0 <https://creativecommons.org/licenses/by-sa/3.0>, via Wikimedia Commons https://commons.wikimedia.org/wiki/File:Ankh_%28SVG%29_01.svg

17 akhenatenator, CC0, via Wikimedia Commons https://commons.wikimedia.org/wiki/File:Faience_%27was%27-sceptre_of_Thuthmosis_III_(8570267204).jpg

18 Jeff Dahl, CC BY-SA 4.0 <https://creativecommons.org/licenses/by-sa/4.0>, via Wikimedia Commons, https://commons.wikimedia.org/wiki/File:Djed.svg

19 T.Voekler, CC BY-SA 3.0 <https://creativecommons.org/licenses/by-sa/3.0>, via Wikimedia Commons, https://commons.wikimedia.org/wiki/File:Detail_of_Nymphaea_%C3%97_daubenyana_W.T.Baxter_ex_Daubeny_flower.jpg

20 https://commons.wikimedia.org/wiki/File:Frankincense_2005-12-31.jpg

21 Ivar Leidus, CC BY-SA 4.0 <https://creativecommons.org/licenses/by-sa/4.0>, via Wikimedia Commons, https://commons.wikimedia.org/wiki/File:Garlic_bulbs_and_cloves.jpg

22 PilotChicago, CC BY-SA 4.0 <https://creativecommons.org/licenses/by-sa/4.0>, via Wikimedia Commons, https://commons.wikimedia.org/wiki/File:Aloe_Vera_houseplant.jpg

23 Evan-Amos, CC0, via Wikimedia Commons, https://commons.wikimedia.org/wiki/File:Thyme-Bundle.jpg

24 https://commons.wikimedia.org/wiki/File:Myrrhe.jpg

25 Analog, Attribution 4.0 International, CC BY 4.0 <https://creativecommons.org/licenses/by/4.0/deed.en> https://www.flickr.com/photos/joostjbakkerijmuiden/51875104830

26 https://commons.wikimedia.org/wiki/File:Baton_de_reglisse.jpg

27 H. Zell, CC BY-SA 3.0 <https://creativecommons.org/licenses/by-sa/3.0>, via Wikimedia Commons, https://commons.wikimedia.org/wiki/File:Chamaemelum_nobile_001.JPG

28 Gary Todd from Xinzheng, China, CC0, via Wikimedia Commons, https://commons.wikimedia.org/wiki/File:Ancient_Egypt_Jewelry,_New_Kingdom_(27798071253).jpg

29 https://commons.wikimedia.org/wiki/File:Egyptian_-_Finger_Ring_with_a_Representation_of_Ptah_-_Walters_42387.jpg

30 Metropolitan Museum of Art, CC0, via Wikimedia Commons, https://commons.wikimedia.org/wiki/File:Necklace_MET_26.7.1379.jpg

31 Getty Villa, CC BY-SA 3.0 <https://creativecommons.org/licenses/by-sa/3.0>, via Wikimedia Commons, https://commons.wikimedia.org/wiki/File:Goldschmuck_-_Diadem.jpg

32 Chapelle musa, CC BY-SA 4.0 <https://creativecommons.org/licenses/by-sa/4.0>, via Wikimedia Commons, https://commons.wikimedia.org/wiki/File:Top_of_Murchision_Falls_on_river_Nile.jpg

33 https://commons.wikimedia.org/wiki/File:African_lions_in_hunting.jpg

34 Giles Laurent, CC BY 4.0 <https://creativecommons.org/licenses/by/4.0>, via Wikimedia Commons, https://commons.wikimedia.org/wiki/File:001_Volcano_eruption_of_Litli-Hr%C3%BAtur_in_Iceland_in_2023_Photo_by_Giles_Laurent.jpg

35 PharaohCrab, CC0, via Wikimedia Commons, https://commons.wikimedia.org/wiki/File:Ptah-Tatenen-Osiris.svg

36 Jon Bodsworth, Copyrighted free use, via Wikimedia Commons, https://commons.wikimedia.org/wiki/File:Pyramidion-satellite-kh%C3%A9ops.jpg

37 SFEC_2009_POT-0008.JPG: S F-E-Cameronderivative work: JMCC1, CC BY-SA 3.0 <https://creativecommons.org/licenses/by-sa/3.0>, via Wikimedia Commons https://commons.wikimedia.org/wiki/File:Ogdoad_-_The_Place_of_Truth_-_Deir_el_Medina.jpg

38 Jeff Dahl, CC BY-SA 4.0 <https://creativecommons.org/licenses/by-sa/4.0>, via Wikimedia Commons, https://commons.wikimedia.org/wiki/File:Re-Horakhty.svg

39 Jeff Dahl, CC BY-SA 4.0 <https://creativecommons.org/licenses/by-sa/4.0>, via Wikimedia Commons, https://commons.wikimedia.org/wiki/File:Standing_Osiris.svg

40 Jeff Dahl, CC BY-SA 4.0 <https://creativecommons.org/licenses/by-sa/4.0>, via Wikimedia Commons, https://commons.wikimedia.org/wiki/File:Isis.svg

41 Jeff Dahl, CC BY-SA 4.0 <https://creativecommons.org/licenses/by-sa/4.0>, via Wikimedia Commons, https://commons.wikimedia.org/wiki/File:Horus_standing.svg

42 Jeff Dahl, CC BY-SA 4.0 <https://creativecommons.org/licenses/by-sa/4.0>, via Wikimedia Commons, https://commons.wikimedia.org/wiki/File:Anubis_standing.svg

43 Jeff Dahl, CC BY-SA 4.0 <https://creativecommons.org/licenses/by-sa/4.0>, via Wikimedia Commons, https://commons.wikimedia.org/wiki/File:Hathor.svg

44 Jeff Dahl, CC BY-SA 4.0 <https://creativecommons.org/licenses/by-sa/4.0>, via Wikimedia Commons, https://commons.wikimedia.org/wiki/File:Sekhmet.svg

45 Jeff Dahl, CC BY-SA 4.0 <https://creativecommons.org/licenses/by-sa/4.0>, via Wikimedia Commons, https://commons.wikimedia.org/wiki/File:Thoth.svg

46 Gunawan Kartapranata, CC BY-SA 3.0 <https://creativecommons.org/licenses/by-sa/3.0>, via Wikimedia Commons, https://commons.wikimedia.org/wiki/File:Bastet.svg

47 Jeff Dahl, CC BY-SA 4.0 <https://creativecommons.org/licenses/by-sa/4.0>, via Wikimedia Commons, https://commons.wikimedia.org/wiki/File:Khepri.svg

48 Jeff Dahl, CC BY-SA 4.0 <https://creativecommons.org/licenses/by-sa/4.0>, via Wikimedia Commons, https://commons.wikimedia.org/wiki/File:Ptah_standing.svg

49 https://commons.wikimedia.org/wiki/File:Heka_god_sm.gif

50 ArchaiOptix, CC BY-SA 4.0 <https://creativecommons.org/licenses/by-sa/4.0>, via Wikimedia Commons https://commons.wikimedia.org/wiki/File:Talatat_block_with_relief_showing_Nefertiti_at_prayer_from_the_temple_of_Aton_at_Karnak_(cropped).jpg

51 Riley Williams, CC BY-SA 4.0 <https://creativecommons.org/licenses/by-sa/4.0>, via Wikimedia Commons, https://commons.wikimedia.org/wiki/File:Private_Kemetic_altar.jpg

52 WikiForMen, CC BY-SA 3.0 <http://creativecommons.org/licenses/by-sa/3.0/>, via Wikimedia Commons, https://commons.wikimedia.org/wiki/File:Compass_Rose_North.svg

53 NASA and The Hubble Heritage Team (AURA/STScI), Public domain, via Wikimedia Commons, https://commons.wikimedia.org/wiki/File:Blackeyegalaxy.jpg

54 Amitchell125, CC BY-SA 4.0 <https://creativecommons.org/licenses/by-sa/4.0>, via Wikimedia Commons, https://commons.wikimedia.org/wiki/File:Ankh_symbols_(on_a_fragment_of_cloth).jpg

55 Walters Art Museum, Public domain, via Wikimedia Commons, https://commons.wikimedia.org/wiki/File:Egyptian_-_Scarab_Amulet_-_Walters_4258_-_Top.jpg

56 Andrew®, CC BY 2.0 <https://creativecommons.org/licenses/by/2.0>, via Wikimedia Commons, https://commons.wikimedia.org/wiki/File:Nile_Flood_plain_limits_(2009).jpg

57 Museo Egizio, CC0, via Wikimedia Commons, https://commons.wikimedia.org/wiki/File:Statuette_of_the_goddess_Isis,_bronze_-_Museo_Egizio_Turin_C_147_p02.jpg

58 Jean-Pierre Dalbéra, CC BY 2.0 <https://creativecommons.org/licenses/by/2.0>, via Wikimedia Commons, https://commons.wikimedia.org/wiki/File:La_tombe_de_Sethi_1er_(KV.17)_(Vall%C3%A9e_des_Rois,_Th%C3%A8bes_ouest)_Solar_barque.jpg

59 Diego Delso, CC BY-SA 4.0 <https://creativecommons.org/licenses/by-sa/4.0>, via Wikimedia Commons, https://commons.wikimedia.org/wiki/File:Templo_funerario_de_Hatshepsut,_Luxor,_Egipto,_2022-04-03,_DD_13.jpg

60 David S. Soriano, CC BY-SA 4.0 <https://creativecommons.org/licenses/by-sa/4.0>, via Wikimedia Commons, https://commons.wikimedia.org/wiki/File:Sweet_Dreams_by_David_S._Soriano.png

61 Anders Sandberg, CC BY 2.0 <https://creativecommons.org/licenses/by/2.0>, via Wikimedia Commons, https://commons.wikimedia.org/wiki/File:Agate_specimen.jpg

62 Gonzalo Devia, CC BY-SA 4.0 <https://creativecommons.org/licenses/by-sa/4.0>, via Wikimedia Commons, https://commons.wikimedia.org/wiki/File:Amatista_Laye_2.jpg

63 Bordercolliez, CC0, via Wikimedia Commons, https://commons.wikimedia.org/wiki/File:Aventurine_1.jpg

64 Romaine, CC0, via Wikimedia Commons, https://commons.wikimedia.org/wiki/File:Leulinghem-calcite_(1).jpg

65 Stephanie Clifford from Arlington, VA, USA, CC BY 2.0 <https://creativecommons.org/licenses/by/2.0>, via Wikimedia Commons, https://commons.wikimedia.org/wiki/File:Carnelian_Quartz_(2932215823).jpg

66 Paweł Maliszczak [hardleo.com], CC BY-SA 4.0 <https://creativecommons.org/licenses/by-sa/4.0>, via Wikimedia Commons, https://commons.wikimedia.org/wiki/File:Rough_Citrine_Cristals_Quartz_from_Brasil.jpg

67 Muséum de Toulouse, CC BY-SA 3.0 <https://creativecommons.org/licenses/by-sa/3.0>, via Wikimedia Commons, https://commons.wikimedia.org/wiki/File:Fluorine_MHNT.MIN.2010.16.1.jpg

68 Rob Lavinsky, iRocks.com – CC-BY-SA-3.0, CC BY-SA 3.0 <https://creativecommons.org/licenses/by-sa/3.0>, via Wikimedia Commons, https://commons.wikimedia.org/wiki/File:Quartz-Hematite-41206.jpg

69 James St. John, CC BY 2.0 <https://creativecommons.org/licenses/by/2.0>, via Wikimedia Commons, https://commons.wikimedia.org/wiki/File:Labradorite_5.jpg

70 W.carter, CC BY-SA 4.0 <https://creativecommons.org/licenses/by-sa/4.0>, via Wikimedia Commons, https://commons.wikimedia.org/wiki/File:Tumble-polished_lapis_lazuli_2.jpg

71 Wouter Hagens, CC BY-SA 4.0 <https://creativecommons.org/licenses/by-sa/4.0>, via Wikimedia Commons, https://commons.wikimedia.org/wiki/File:Moonstone_B.jpg

72 Bryan Barnes, CC BY-SA 4.0 <https://creativecommons.org/licenses/by-sa/4.0>, via Wikimedia Commons, https://commons.wikimedia.org/wiki/File:NM_Selenite_Crystal_Cluster.jpg

73 James St. John, CC BY 2.0 <https://creativecommons.org/licenses/by/2.0>, via Wikimedia Commons, https://commons.wikimedia.org/wiki/File:Schorl_tourmaline_7.jpg

74 Serg Childed, CC BY-SA 4.0 <https://creativecommons.org/licenses/by-sa/4.0>, via Wikimedia Commons, https://commons.wikimedia.org/wiki/File:Singing_Bowl_from_Nepal.jpg

75 Reinhold Möller, CC BY-SA 4.0 <https://creativecommons.org/licenses/by-sa/4.0>, via Wikimedia Commons, https://commons.wikimedia.org/wiki/File:Nezu_Museum_Gong-20091020-RM-111948.jpg

76 K.Venkataramana, CC0, via Wikimedia Commons, https://commons.wikimedia.org/wiki/File:Tuning_forks_-_Various_frequencies.jpg

77 kallerna, CC BY-SA 3.0 <https://creativecommons.org/licenses/by-sa/3.0>, via Wikimedia Commons, https://commons.wikimedia.org/wiki/File:Sphinx_and_pyramids_of_Giza_panorama.jpg

78 User:Life of Riley, CC BY-SA 3.0 <https://creativecommons.org/licenses/by-sa/3.0>, via Wikimedia Commons, https://commons.wikimedia.org/wiki/File:Flower-of-Life-small.svg

79 Mandalasheets, CC0, via Wikimedia Commons, https://commons.wikimedia.org/wiki/File:Sun-Mandala-Element.jpg

80 Andonee, CC BY-SA 4.0 <https://creativecommons.org/licenses/by-sa/4.0>, via Wikimedia Commons https://commons.wikimedia.org/wiki/File:Moon_Phase_Diagram_for_Simple_English_Wikipedia.GIF

81 Henrysz, CC BY 4.0 <https://creativecommons.org/licenses/by/4.0>, via Wikimedia Commons, https://commons.wikimedia.org/wiki/File:Allegory_of_Justice_with_the_Coat_of_Arms_of_Anthoni_Wyss_Detail_1.jpg

82 Museo Egizio, Turin, CC0, via Wikimedia Commons, https://commons.wikimedia.org/wiki/File:Kha_and_Merit_before_Osiris_Book_of_the_Dead_of_Kha.jpg

83 Diego Delso, CC BY-SA 4.0 <https://creativecommons.org/licenses/by-sa/4.0>, via Wikimedia Commons, https://commons.wikimedia.org/wiki/File:File,_Asu%C3%A1n,_Egipto,_2022-04-01,_DD_144.jpg

84 WSP300, CC0, via Wikimedia Commons, https://commons.wikimedia.org/wiki/File:Ancient_Egyptian_Vexilloids_in_Tomb_Paintings_1.webp

www.ingramcontent.com/pod-product-compliance
Lightning Source LLC
Chambersburg PA
CBHW051831160426
43209CB000 06B/1128